HEADS
AND
TAILS

HEADS AND TAILS

Following and Leading in Kingdom-Formed Organizations

Richard Kriegbaum

invite
PRESS
Plano, Texas

The world has now become the Kingdom of our Lord and of his Christ,
and he will reign forever and ever.
—Revelation 11:15

Make the Kingdom of God your primary concern.
—Luke 12:31 NLT

May your kingdom come soon.
May your will be done on earth,
as it is in heaven.
—Matthew 6:10

Contents

Contents

Doing Effectiveness

Preface

We were made for heaven. In the Kingdom of God, there is no difference between the status or worth of the followership and leadership sides of the organizational coin. Jesus Christ came from heaven to earth as God in human form to announce and explain the Kingdom of God and invite people to follow him as their one true King. He says to pray to the Father in Heaven for the Kingdom to come soon, for God's will to be done on earth as it is in heaven. He tells his followers to seek the Kingdom of God above all else, to "make the Kingdom of God your primary concern" in all of life, now on the fallen earth as it is in the perfection of heaven.

In this process, your King Jesus is your personal model; you are to become more like Jesus who sacrificed himself so rebellious humans could be reconciled to God. Similarly, the organizations of the Kingdom of God are the model and ideal for all your earthly organizations: church, family, work, educational, political. The coin of every organization has two interdependent and equally important sides, following and leading.

You are to help form all your earthly organizations to be more like the organizations of the heavenly realm of God's Kingdom.

The two sides of the organizational "coin" define each other. A leader has followers who accept the influence of the leader (in varying ways and degrees). If you cannot find any followership, don't bother looking for leadership. Under Christ the King, wise and effective followers in every kind of organization choose, support, and evaluate leaders who demonstrate competency and deserve trust in both roles, following and leading. Followership and leadership define each other and operate interdependently to advance shared organizational purposes. From nuclear families to governments and multinational corporations, Jesus offered his followers no exceptions: seek first the Kingdom of God, and your heavenly Father will give you all you need.

But the dominant culture is leader-centric, and Satan likes it that way. He was a bright leader with great authority in the angelic armies, but he did not want to be under the authority of God or anyone else, so he led a rebellion, and God cast him and his followers down to the earthly realm. There he craftily deceived Eve to feel like she was her own leader and not be demeaned as a mere follower under God's authority. Leadership continues to be treated as the only side of the organizational coin that really matters in our earthly socio-economic system. Everyone else is "just a follower."

Kingdom-formed organizations under God's sovereignty recognize that the followership role is the primal force in all organizations. Effective following determines who leads and ultimately how successful they will be in their leadership role. This book intends to inform, enhance, and encourage the effectiveness of interdependent followership and leadership that moves the organizations you are part of toward the character, values, and conditions of God's Kingdom on earth.

When Christ the King returns with power, earth and heaven will be unified in one glorious kingdom with healthy people practicing effective following and leading forever as Christ-like servants in healthy organizations under his rule and for his glory. For now, the obvious challenge is that, in this fallen world, unhealthy leadership fits the fallen human ego better than healthy servant-followership. Humans are easily attracted to unhealthy leaders. In kingdom-formed organizations the followership is fully engaged in ensuring the effective leadership required to achieve their shared purpose and values.

PART 1

Seeing What Is Not Obvious

Seeing What Your Vision Makes Invisible

They brought me in here to be a visionary leader, but nobody here knows how to follow." The departing CEO spoke in the hearing of the few staff who provided his administrative support but to no person in particular. His chief executive leadership position had ended prematurely and without ceremony. He offered his explanation to make some plausible sense of a failed effort that was heavy with loss for him and for the whole organization. He offered it as a characterization that he could live with, a plausible logic of why everything had so rapidly and undeniably fallen apart.

As the door closed from the office to the hallway, a woman who had helped give him administrative support spoke quietly, also to no person in particular: "I wonder if he includes himself with all the people here who don't know how to follow."

Instead of the desired turnaround and renewal, the whole situation had gone from bad to worse. Failed leadership in all kinds of organizations is so common that it no longer requires any substantive explanation. Many such executive departures are covered with a severance payment and shrouded with the mutually binding opacity of nondisclosure agreements that prevent the candid discussion and analysis that should characterize a Christian community and that could promote learning, healing, and healthy closure.

Vision is essential. One of the highest priority expectations of the leadership role is instilling a compelling vision of the desired organizational future. That future vision rests on the foundation of an accurate shared vision of the current reality of the organization, its starting point conditions. Any such vision—current or future—must exclude some elements and include others. The excluded factors cannot be important, so they become invisible. Soon they are not part of the corporate culture or conversation. Then they are forgotten, and eventually they do not exist. This selective blindness is necessary for any vision. But when a mission-critical element like informed and effective followership is lost, the resulting distortions are insidiously invisible.

The invisible power of effective followership is easily lost.

One of the main reasons you have leaders is to have someone to blame if the vision of the current reality is incorrect or the future vision is not wise or is not achieved. If the organization fails, the logic goes, you cannot blame and replace all the people in the organization. Instead, you blame and replace one or more members of the top leadership. In exchange for this solution, you agree to give the leader credit for any successes, even when the outcomes are the product of the total organizational effort to which the leader may have contributed little or nothing. You even allow the leader implicit credit for favorable outside events that "just happen," partly on the assumption that the right leader seems to attract such good fortune.

But for this departing CEO, there had been no saving surprises, and the corporate vision of the existing reality remained a collection of conflicting and often mutually exclusive visions driven by selected facts, special interests, and quasi-sacred institutional mythology. The leader's vision of the current reality was merely one of many extant descriptions of the current condition. There had been a great deal more speaking than listening. The leader was departing, without accusing any particular person or group by name. Instead, he shifted the burden of responsibility from a particular failure of leadership to a systemic failure of followership that included unanticipated resistance to change, even when it was widely agreed that change was urgently needed for survival and success. Followership factors had not been part of the consideration when he was hired. Followership was not an explicit element of the organizational self-description, and it was not part of the desired future vision.

He departed not believing that he had been the primary cause of the failure, even though he accepted the reality that it is one of the normal and customary ways to frame such corporate events. He was not accusing the organization of overtly rebelling or refusing to accept his direction, even though there certainly had been resistance to many of the unwelcome changes he believed were necessary.

As he saw it, the organization simply did not know how to accept and support a transformational leader with a bold vision of a dramatically different future for the organization. He believed the organization had too many ineffective followers, competing leaders, and conflicting values. From his perspective, he had done what an effective leader must do, but too many people had failed to do what followers must do. The organization had welcomed him with high hopes and a sense of organizational urgency that magnified the need for him to succeed. His previous leadership successes had brought hope and energy. Euphoria made doubtful followers agree to hold their concerns and wait hopefully in good faith.

But higher hopes led to deeper disappointment when hope faded. Publicly he handled the situation with professional grace. Privately he blamed the members of the organization for not following well. Some in the organization believed he had not been treated fairly. Others thought he had failed to listen and learn, so that he could understand and respect the organizational culture and values, either because no one mentored him on that reality or because he saw that reality as the primary cause of the crisis and tried to rapidly replace it. But no one noted the absence of an adequately shared vision of their current reality in which their followership was simply assumed.

The board concluded that their only option was to change leadership, but the lack of a shared vision of the present organizational reality remained. A central factor in that unseen reality was the absence of effective following. The board did not see the impact of their own ignorance of effective following in their organizational governance. As the formal leaders, they assumed that, because they were in agreement about the urgency of the situation, all the organizational followers would "follow as usual" and do everything needed for the new leader to succeed. But the followers were not in adequate agreement about what the organizational condition was or about the priorities for the future, so they remained silent.

It is difficult to notice something that is just quietly missing, something real and relevant but recognized, something essential that simply is not there. What you cannot see soon does not exist, and what is not real is, understandably, not a factor in your decisions. The absence of a shared current vision is easy to miss, partly because people of goodwill and kindly disposition often find ways to relate and work together despite unresolved differences. It is easy for the primal power of followership to be completely missing from any organizational vision, whether it is the present reality or a vision of the desired future.

Meditation

> As Jesus and the disciples left the town of Jericho, a large crowd followed behind. Two blind men were sitting beside the road. When they heard that Jesus was coming that way, they began shouting, "Lord, son of David, have mercy on us!"
>
> . . . When Jesus heard them, he stopped and called, "What do you want me to do for you?" "Lord," they said, "we want to see!" Jesus felt sorry for them and touched their eyes. Instantly they could see! Then they followed him. (Matthew 20:29–34)

Every type of leadership depends on having its corresponding type of followership. Visionary leadership depends on the vision of followership. When a vision is shared, the divine light shines on the leader and the followers together as they find their way forward. Acknowledging blindness is the first step toward seeing, just as humbly acknowledging ignorance is the first step toward wisdom.

Talking with God

> *Lord, have mercy on me. Your vision is perfect, but mine is so distorted, fragmented, and filtered that often I cannot even agree with my colleagues about what we should look at or look for. And too often they are no better at it than I am. So, when we do manage to look at the same situation, we do not see the same things. If our shared blindness were physical, it would be more obvious that we need you to heal us. But in my willful certainty I am sure that I see things correctly, and that everyone else seems to be strangely blind to the obvious truth. I can't blame them for treating me the same way.*
>
> *Lord, have mercy on us. We need to see a shared spiritual vision of our present reality and the future we hope for. We each have selective vision. Unless your Spirit shows us what the whole vision looks like, we*

have no hope of reaching the same distant goal together. We are blind and do not know it. Heal us. With you all things are possible. Touch our eyes so we can see ourselves and our situation as you see them and follow each other forward on your pathway for us. Amen.

Questions and Issues

A. Since an organizational vision is inherently selective by its purpose, how could an organization maximize its collective wisdom by seeing and intentionally selecting the "invisible" elements they want and do not want in their shared vision?

B. What other important vision elements tend to be invisible like followership?

C. How can you make an invisible but critical organizational element—like effective followership—be visible and relevant?

CHAPTER 2

Seeing What a Culture Makes Invisible

The explanation of the CEO as he finished would have been more accurate and more useful if he had said, "You brought me in here to be a visionary leader, but nobody here knew how to follow *me*. We were all preoccupied with leadership, but not enough of us—me included—really knew how to follow each other well enough to find our shared wisdom and get the job done. I did not follow or lead effectively."

The entire organizational event becomes more understandable if the conceptual frame is broadened to include the elements of failed followership in the organizational reality, none of which was adequately apparent to the followers who were responsible for choosing their leader and ensuring his success:

- Despite his leadership experience and charisma, the skills of other supporting leaders, and the motivation of an urgent situation, not nearly enough people in the organization had chosen to actively follow and support his leadership.

- The lack of effective followership had made all leadership in the organization less effective than was required when they faced an extreme challenge with insufficient time to learn from each other and change.

- The concept that skillful leading is learned was broadly assumed, and leaders were intentionally developed and rewarded. But followership was assumed to be common sense, passive compliance, and dependent upon personality type.

- Many people had been taught to lead but almost none had been taught how to fully engage in effective following, so they did not really know how to support leadership in general, and this CEO's form of bold leadership in particular. Therefore, they could not contribute well enough for his leadership to advance the health and success of the organization.

- In his visionary leading he did not listen, learn, or follow very well, even as the counsel from a few key followers became more specific and urgent.

The fragility of the organization when he assumed his leadership responsibility needed an unusually high level of effectiveness in dynamic, collaborative following and leading that few organizations master and that he personally had not observed or learned to do.

He was a capable leader who moved on to success in other assignments and settings. But he left behind a vulnerable organization that was still in decline and jeopardized on most indicators of viability. The toxic situation that leaders and followers at all levels of the organization had unwittingly colluded to create was so severe that the organization remained vulnerable for several more years. Some people left, including board members, but gradually a culture of engaged following emerged.

Every organization develops a culture with values and patterns of behavior that help define who they are and that structure how they function together. That culture makes certain things more important and thus more visible, and it makes other elements of reality less important and thus less visible. Such selection is essential to organizational differentiation and identity. Agreement about what matters and what does not matter is essential to define organizational values. Over time, whoever or whatever is unimportant is filtered out of the reality of the organization, becomes invisible, is not mentioned, and, in practice, ceases to exist.

Homeless people provide a convincing example of this principle. Most cities have people who do not have decent, safe, stable housing. In most cases, homelessness is a result of financial poverty, and these two coexisting conditions typically indicate or produce several other associated issues of human suffering ranging from abuse and addictions through mental health issues and spiritual hopelessness. Sometimes it is crisis-driven and temporary, and sometimes it is chronic, for the homeless and for the city. Often

7

the homeless hide at the edges of urban life and go unnoticed, filtered out of the picture. Sometimes there is no place for them to hide, so other solutions are found.

Such human conditions are uncomfortable and even offensive for most people to see, so considerable effort is expended to make homelessness invisible. The result is that your poor and homeless neighbors, whom Christ instructed you to love as you love yourself, become your invisible neighbors. In some factually objective way, you know that these homeless neighbors exist. You wish them no harm. In fact, you would like them to have a better life, and you may even donate to organizations that do see those homeless people every day, that seek to minister to them on your behalf, and that help them move toward hope and human flourishing. The culture seeks ways to make the homeless invisible.

The principle is simply that every organization, including your city, your church, and the one you work for or own, has a culture, and its culture makes certain things important and obvious, while making other things less important and unobvious. When this filtering and prioritizing process is highly successful, it ultimately makes lower priorities invisible and then, in practice, nonexistent.

You have watched young children delight in the simple game of hiding an object behind your back. Child psychologists explain that what makes this activity such giggling fun for the child is that the object actually goes out of existence until it is brought back into view and magically becomes real again. Most people mature into understanding "object permanence" so that even things that may not be currently visible do exist and are possibly extremely important—things like your homeless neighbors, an undesirable part of your marriage, a challenging friendship, or the Kingdom of God—these may be invisible at times, but they really do exist.

Similarly, followership tends to be an invisible element of organizational life. It is typically easy to see the leaders and their roles and effects. But it is just as easy if not more common to not see or recognize the decisive contributions of people who perform the behind the scenes work of following, *and* to miss the dynamic reciprocity of following and leading.

If you are leading, that makes you important, and you enjoy high status. Leaders deserve professional development to help them lead well. But when you are following, the dominant culture silently says that you are less important, you have no special status, and you are not deserving or in need of intentional development to follow more effectively. As a follower, you are commonly considered as part of an invisible organizational element that is created and controlled by the leaders.

Jesus sees things differently. He sees you doing what he told you to do. He sees you following and not just following him but wisely choosing and actively supporting the persons that he wants you to follow as you seek first the coming of his Kingdom.

Meditation

Therefore, listen to this message from the Lord, you scoffing rulers in Jerusalem. You boast, "We have struck a bargain to cheat death and have made a deal to dodge the grave. The coming destruction can never touch us, for we have built a strong refuge made of lies and deception." (Isaiah 28:14-15)

How easy it is to let the world squeeze you into its model and conform your values to its assumptions and priorities. How natural it feels in that dominant culture to focus entirely on leaders and leading, the people with power and status. And how natural it feels to operate in practice as though all the work of following just sort of happens somehow, as the magic of leadership creates what matters, what exists, and what you can see and value. But deception can never protect you from destruction. Fake leaders, fake information, false assumptions, false accusations, and flawed values produce very real human disasters.

Talking with God

Heavenly Father, I talk with you from my heart as sincerely and honestly as I know how, but my feelings are flawed by my fears, even though you constantly remind me not to be afraid. My view of you is too small, and my perception of reality is too easily distorted by my constant efforts to respect the cultures and psyches of the people I serve. I know I become selectively blinded to what is real and what truly matters most, without even being aware of it.

I am much better at seeing the ignorance, weaknesses, and failures of other people than I am at seeing my own faults and blunders. How easily I blame others when things go wrong and forget that my vision of reality always has blind spots where my frame of reference screens out elements that don't fit. I can lie to myself without being aware of my deception. I am so often not even aware that I am ignorant. I depend on your Holy Spirit to teach me how to pray, and to make my words express what is true, honorable, and right.

I come to you, Father, frustrated that the people I try to serve with faithful following or leading seem determined to ignore what it seems you have shown me for their benefit. Open their eyes Lord, but also open mine, so we can learn together and find a fuller shared vision of our current reality and what might truly be possible for us in the future. I want to see the whole picture as you see it, including my own failures as I try to follow and lead those you have entrusted to me. When I am following and when I am leading, heal my blindness, Lord. I want eyes of faith and kingdom vision for all of us to see what you see and want what you want for us. Amen.

Questions and Issues

A. What are some of the ways that the cultural values of a nation, a geographic region, a faith community, or a political party make things seem visible that do not really exist as depicted?

B. What are examples of making uncomfortable or unpopular realities unimportant or invisible?

C. What are some examples of potentially valuable elements of an organizational culture that have been intentionally devalued and made invisible?

D. How can followership become more visible, integral, and effective in the life of a traditionally leader-centric organization?

E. In what situations could it be counterproductive to increase the visibility and effectiveness of followership in an organization?

The Essential Role of Organizations in God's Plan

Y ou are an organizational person because you are a relational person. God made you that way on purpose, in his image, for relationship with him. It is no accident that organizations are ubiquitous and that you are connected with so many organizations. They are a major part of God's design for all persons in his created order, including both humans and angels. Even though Adam was created sinless in the image of God and was placed in a perfect environment in the garden of Eden and was an intimate conversational friend of God, the Creator declared that it is not good for a person to be alone. Human life is fundamentally and necessarily framed and pursued in various personal relationships and organized social units.

The existence of organizations is universal across all human cultures. This is true on earth now, and it will continue to be true on the New Earth of the perfected Kingdom of God that is yet to come. On the fallen earth that we experience now, all human organizations are fundamentally flawed by sinful rebellion, but human organizations are honorable and essential expressions of God's plan for humanity. Like the rest of creation, organizations need divine redemption to properly serve their Creator and the humans made in their Creator's image. Organizations are essential in the divine order of creation.

That is why it is not possible to be fully human without being engaged with an organization, and in a technologically advanced society, you are enmeshed with more organizations than you can possibly be aware of. Some of them are obvious to you; they are visible. Some are not obvious; they are invisible. Over time, any person or thing that is invisible ceases to exist for you. This largely explains the prevalence of physical idols in many religions, and phenomena like the deification of earthly rulers as the Romans, Egyptians, and others practiced, and as some nations do now. An invisible God does not feel real to physical humans on a physical earth. Thus, God gave us the one and only true Son of God who was also Son of Man. "Christ is the visible image of the invisible God" (Col 1:15). Some organizations are inherently visible, and some are invisible. God's created order includes both kinds of organizations, now and in the Kingdom of Heaven to come.

The basic definition of an organization is consistent in all situations: Any group of people identified by a shared interest or purpose is an organization. Managing your complex and pervasive system of visible and invisible organizations is a daunting challenge, but if you are a follower of Jesus to any significant degree, you have an even greater challenge that involves two organizations that are related to each other but separate and distinct. They are both related to all your other organizations, but they are also separate and distinct from those. Jesus Christ is the head of two gigantic super-organizations that you automatically belong to as his follower: his Church and his Kingdom. He is also the head of a gigantic and extremely powerful organization of angels, sometimes called the Angelic Army, that operates in heaven and on earth. Jesus may have other organizations that we do not know about, because his Kingdom includes all of what we call the natural creation.

Any group of people identified by a shared interest or purpose is an organization.

In his Kingdom, he is the king and you are a citizen and servant of the king. This Kingdom also includes the organization of the angelic persons. Angels are real, but angels are rarely visible to humans and are only seen and recognized under special circumstances and for limited times. The Kingdom of Christ is very real but it is not obvious. In your normal daily life, it is invisible.

Your other super-organization is his Church, where he is the head and you are a member, a living part of his body, the "body of Christ" on earth. The Church and the Angelic Army are two major and separate organizations within the Kingdom of Christ. The Church and the Kingdom are not just different names for the same thing. The Church is part of the Kingdom, essentially an organization within an organization, and so is the Angelic Army. The Church is the core strategy of the King for humans to do what he wants accomplished in his Kingdom on earth during this period of time when he is physically absent, between his first coming to earth and when he will return to fully implement his absolute reign over a new earth.

The Church is naturally and appropriately understood to be all the various groups—commonly referred to as congregations or local churches—that gather for corporate worship, fellowship, instruction and training, support, telling the good news, and making disciples of Jesus Christ. Many of these activities are advanced by purposeful suborganizations that operate within a local church or congregation and for the benefit of the members of that congregation. Most congregations also create their own suborganizations to facilitate effective outreach to help meet the spiritual, physical, social, or emotional needs of persons outside the congregation.

Groups or associations of local churches, generically referred to as denominations, often organize around commonalities such as doctrinal beliefs, ministries and services, culture, race, ethnicity, language, location, and other factors. Many organizations that are commonly called parachurch organizations are created and sustained by the Church to advance its kingdom commission in every conceivable area of human experience from birth to death. These organizations include hospitals, universities, print and digital media, biblical translation, addiction recovery, parenting preschoolers, community development, restorative justice, evangelism, hunger, housing, mental health, peacemaking, finance, and investments. Altogether they are an uncountable list of organizations with an uncountable list of human services. Some are legally incorporated and sometimes even partially funded by the government of one or more nations; some are tiny and hardly noticed by anyone. They are not a local church, congregation, or denomination, but they are supported by the Church, and they exist to advance the kingdom mission of the Church. Taken together worldwide, the Church and all its organizational extensions are the global faith community of the Kingdom of God. That conglomerate is sometimes referred to as Christendom. You only see small parts of it.

Meditation

When the king of Aram was at war with Israel, he would confer with his officers and say, "We will mobilize our forces at such and such a place." But immediately Elisha, the man of God, would warn the king of Israel. . . . The king of Aram became very upset over this. He called his officers together and demanded, "Which of you is the traitor?"

"It's not us, my lord the king," one of the officers replied. "Elisha, the prophet in Israel, tells the king of Israel even the words you speak in the privacy of your bedroom!"

"Go and find out where he is," the king commanded, "so I can send troops to seize him." And the report came back: "Elisha is at Dothan." So, one night the king of Aram sent a great army with many chariots and horses to surround the city. When the servant of the man of God got up early the next morning and went outside, there were troops, horses, and chariots everywhere. "Oh, sir, what will we do now?" the young man cried to Elisha.

"Don't be afraid!" Elisha told him "For there are more on our side than on theirs!" Then Elisha prayed, "Oh Lord, open his eyes and let him see!" The Lord opened the young man's eyes, and when he looked up, he saw that the hillside around Elisha was filled with horses and chariots of fire. (II Kings 6:8-17)

The Angelic Army is a gigantic and enormously powerful organization in God's Kingdom that is constantly at work, but presently it is almost always invisible on earth. Whether you are following or leading, and in every kind of organizational situation, you can enjoy the courage that comes from knowing that you are not alone in trying to advance the Church or the Kingdom of God on earth. In addition to the Spirit of God alive in you, powerful unseen forces are at work in response to prayers, faith-based vision, and action to do what is right in response to the call and promises of God.

Talking with God

Teach me to see the things and the people that the world around me trains me to ignore. Teach me to see the organizations and powers that I miss because I have adopted the values and priorities of the culture around me.

Teach me to appreciate the whole range of organizations that I often do not recognize as part of your creation and your ultimate purposes. Teach me to believe that you are at work in every organizational situation even when I cannot see all the ways you are active. Teach me to glimpse what you are up to. Give me the courage and wisdom to act for your Church and to understand what advances your Kingdom, especially when spiritual realities are so invisible and I feel so clueless and powerless. I need vision and hope from you. Amen.

Questions and Issues

A. What are some of the ways that the cultural values of a nation, geographic region, faith community, or political party have made some things seem visible that do not really exist as they are depicted and/or made certain uncomfortable or unpopular realities unimportant or invisible?

B. What are some examples of potentially valuable elements of an organizational culture that have been intentionally devalued and made invisible?

C. How can followership become more visible, integral, and effective in the life of a traditionally leader-centric organization?

D. In what situations could it be counterproductive to increase the visibility and effectiveness of followership in an organization?

Seeing the Invisible Kingdom

You depend on organizations of all kinds for most of the things that really matter. From food for the body to food for the soul, and from how you make a living to how you live like Christ in the world, organized human activity plays a role in almost every aspect of human existence in every country on earth. The impact that all these organizations have on your life makes you aware that they are important to you. Because they are important to many people, they are highly visible. Naturally, you want your organizations to serve human needs and interests as well as possible, including your own needs. You want them to be healthy organizations that serve people well and succeed financially.

The particulars of each organizational story are highly variable, but the underlying principles and patterns of healthy and unhealthy organizational life are consistent. The clear priority from Jesus is to make the Kingdom of God your top priority and primary concern, and that includes all your organizations. But the research, literature, theories, and books from the leadership gurus make it very tempting to ignore the kingdom perspective and convince yourself that the Kingdom of God is only a spiritual phenomenon now, a matter of the heart, not a matter of corporate priorities, practices, and policies.

The dominant culture of the world can squeeze your mind and spirit into its model because it can satisfy some of your needs. You find what you want on the Internet and it is delivered to your door. It is a well-organized system of organizations, and it works well enough if you do things its way and follow its messages. You must tell the system what it needs to know, and give it what it requires, including what it wants to know about you. That information helps that massive system provide what you want.

But as countless mostly small and harmless accommodations accumulate, culture-induced blindness too easily predominates and makes it impossible to see by faith a mostly invisible Kingdom of God. Indeed, that amazing system of very visible organizations may seem to have almost nothing to do with your call to be a servant-follower of Jesus, your invisible King. "You love him even though you have never seen him. Though you do not see him now, you trust him; and you rejoice with a glorious inexpressible joy" (1 Peter 1:8).

By faith you are a steward of the very tangible kingdom resources of an otherwise invisible Kingdom with an invisible King. You are a prophetic witness for the invisible Kingdom that will someday become a wondrously visible reality when the King you love, trust, and worship returns with visible power and glory. Your mandate from your King applies regardless of what organizational context you are called to work in or do business with: secular, Christian, for-profit, nonprofit, governmental, church, incorporated, informal, or family. Make the Kingdom of Christ your controlling priority.

Your kingdom priority could seem downright stupid or simply impossible if you work for a company that often implements policies or practices that contradict the values of the Kingdom of God. Thinking "kingdom first" is countercultural and does not happen naturally or easily. The two worldviews seem to be two unconnected spheres of reality.

Yet Jesus says, "Your Father already knows your needs. He will give you all you need from day to day if you make the Kingdom of God your primary concern" (Luke 12:30-31 NLT). Make it your top priority in every plan, policy, and program; in every transaction, relationship, communication, and performance evaluation. Do it in every sale, every purchase, every personnel hire, every capital investment, every report, every joke, every marketing message, every product development, every element of customer service management, every part of everything.

It easily seems impossible to envision making the Kingdom of God your primary concern so that you think, speak, and act with primacy for the Kingdom. You could naturally conclude that any organization in any sector of the socioeconomic complex that might try to be truly Kingdom-like in the spiritual and moral darkness of the real world would be overwhelmed by the competition and driven out of organizational existence. And you might naturally conclude that any one person who tried to move toward the ideal of being Christlike and nudge an organization toward the Kingdom of Christ would sooner or later be severely disadvantaged and be moved aside or released.

How can your King righteously hold you accountable for praying and working for his Kingdom to come here and now in this world as it is in heaven? What can you justifiably be expected to do as one lone person to make the Kingdom of Jesus Christ your primary concern, especially if you find yourself in the context of a godless organization operating with godless values in a godless economy and culture for godless outcomes? How can you rightly be expected to serve the values and purposes of a kingdom that is invisible to everyone else? How can you be confident in your own ability to see the invisible Kingdom of Jesus Christ and make it your core priority and your organizational model?

The error of thinking of the eternal life to come in heaven in narrowly spiritualized terms with resurrected persons in an endless worship service can prevent Christians from understanding what Jesus means when he tells them to "make the Kingdom of God your highest priority" on earth right now. Author Randy Alcorn puts it this way: "Those who imagine that spirituality is something ethereal and invisible—unrelated to our physical skills, creativity, and cultural development—fail to understand Scripture. . . . God is a maker. He'll never cease being a maker. God made us, his image bearers, to be makers. We'll never cease to be makers."[1] Alcorn describes eternal life in heaven on the New Earth in the Kingdom of God as "a physical environment with physical people who work, eat, converse, and hold positions of authority. People live both inside and outside the city, come into each other's homes, travel, and worship together. Leaders of nations will bring the splendor of different cultures into the city where Jesus Christ will reign on the throne."[2]

Alcorn believes that "we will see trade and business in Heaven, although not for all the same reasons we engage in them now." They could be parts of a "social structure centered on creating, giving, and receiving," not out of human need or sin but out of "human interdependence, creativity, and variety." On the New Earth you should expect to find tables, chairs, wagons, machinery, transportation, sports equipment . . . technology . . . a computer." Under the rule of its King, Jesus Christ, the Kingdom of God will include a new earth on which to worship and glorify God by learning, serving, and creating together in well organized "satisfying and enriching work."[3]

You will enter that new life with the knowledge and skills you developed on the earth under the curse. So, the closer you come to that kingdom ideal now, the better it is now and in the life to come. There will be organizations with leading and following but with no status differential between those roles and with an eternity to learn and work. To make the Kingdom of Christ your primary concern now, you learn to see the true reality of the future Kingdom with spiritual vision, and you learn to support it everywhere it already exists or can be advanced in your world now. The first step is to really and truly want it.

Meditation

As Jesus was walking along, he saw a man who had been blind from birth. . . ."It was not because of his sins or his parents' sins," Jesus answered. "He was born blind so the power of God could be seen in him." . . . Then he spit on the ground, made mud with the saliva, and smoothed the mud over the blind man's eyes. He told him, "Go and wash in the pool of Siloam.". . . So, the man went and washed, and came back seeing!

His neighbors and others who knew him as a blind beggar . . . asked, "Who healed you? What happened?" He told them, "The man they call Jesus. . . ." Then they took the man to the Pharisees. . . .The Pharisees asked the man all about it. . . . "Give glory to God by telling the truth, because we know Jesus is a sinner."

"I don't know whether he is a sinner," the man replied. "But I know this: I was blind, and now I can see!" . . . And they threw him out of the synagogue.

. . . When Jesus heard what had happened, he found the man and said, "Do you believe in the Son of Man?" The man answered, "Who is he, sir, because I would like to."

"You have seen him," Jesus said, "and he is speaking to you!"

"Yes, Lord," the man said, "I believe!" And he worshiped Jesus.

Then Jesus told him, "I have come to judge the world. I have come to give sight to the blind and to show those who think they see that they are blind." (John 9:1-39 NLT)

The first step toward a shared vision is the admission of blindness, and the second step is a sincere desire to be healed and see what was previously not visible to you. Jesus gives sight when you admit you cannot see, even something as simple as seeing another person's way of seeing, and he grants blindness to those who are too proud to admit that they cannot see.

Pride is blinding and binding. True humility welcomes new vision and new freedom.

Talking with God

God of light, you are invisible, but you see and know everything perfectly. I worship you with a grateful heart for saying "let there be light" and making it so. Jesus Christ, light of the world, thank you for coming to rescue your children from the kingdom of darkness. I ask that by your grace we will all walk together in the light of "a complete understanding of what (you) want to do in (our) lives," and see what others see so that together we can be "wise with spiritual wisdom" (Col. 1:9 NLT). Let it be so, Lord Jesus. And let it be soon.

Questions and Issues

A. What are the most convincing points to support the idea that the instruction of Jesus to "seek first the Kingdom of God" refers only to the personal life experience and service of those who seek by faith to follow Jesus while waiting for the visible Kingdom to come?

B. What are the most convincing points that support the concept that followers of Jesus are supposed to work actively to advance kingdom values and conditions in the tangible, visible affairs of this world, including in its secular organizations and political systems?

C. What are the most important characteristics of a healthy organization?

D. Why do so many organizations measure success by financial profits for the owners and executive leaders at the expense of subordinate employee followers?

The One Most Important Organization

J esus has given his followers an all-inclusive principle to properly order and evaluate everything you do, including every organizational entity and activity and every relationship. There are no exclusions, caveats, or provisos. If you want God to give you what you need to survive and thrive in this earthly life, then Jesus says to always follow this core principle and seek this outcome in every part of your life, including every kind of organizational setting, situation, or relationship.

Make the Kingdom of God your primary concern. Seek the Kingdom of God above all else. Seek first the Kingdom of God.

One of your smallest but most important organizations to make like God's Kingdom may be your nuclear or extended family, which can be as small as a married couple or a parent and a child. On the other end of the continuum of organizational size and complexity is a nation in which you have citizenship, which could have hundreds of millions of members with conflicting cultures and political parties and feel totally beyond your influence as it determines what you must do, may do, and may not do. Larger and possibly even more challenging could be your relationship to one of the world religions, which could have billions of members in many nations. And across all continents, cultures, countries, and religions there are giant multinational corporations. In every case, you are to make the Kingdom of God your primary concern as you relate to them.

You belong in highly varied ways to countless organizations. You may belong to some organizations and be oppressed by others. You may be a member of a business corporation where you make a living; a local church congregation where you fellowship, worship, learn, serve, and donate your time and money; a jury that decides a person's guilt or innocence and then disbands; an athletic team that you play on or cheer for; various schools, where you belong to student, alumni, parent, trustee, or donor groups; a tax exempt public benefit corporation that you may support with donations of time, talent, and treasure; a neighborhood association; a political party; a giant discount retail organization, or the local fitness center where you work out. But in every case, you are to make the Kingdom of God your primary concern, your guiding priority.

In addition to all the varied organizations that you belong to in one way or another, your life is also powerfully and deeply connected to countless other organizations on which your life and welfare depend. Your birth typically happens in a healthcare organization that informs an agency of state government when you come into existence as one of its member citizens, and your final remains will be cared for by a funeral organization that informs the state that one of its member citizens has died. From birth to death, you are the center of your particular web of organizations. Each one affects you in various ways and you affect them, sometimes minutely and sometimes profoundly. In everything they do to you and for you, and in everything you do to and for each of them, your assignment from your king always applies. Put Christ's Kingdom first. Make Christ's Kingdom your top priority. Make the Kingdom of God your primary concern, your first thought, your core controlling priority in all of life, including every relationship, and every one of your organizations.

The Kingdom of God is a unique organization.

The obvious challenge of seeking first the Kingdom of God is that it is not obvious. Without a physically visible leader in the earthly realm, how do you have a real organization to which you can give top priority? Even when the King himself was visibly and tangibly present with his followers on earth as the promised Messiah, they could not comprehend its reality if

it was not immediately visible with the physical reality, power, and authority of a normal kingdom on earth.

Jesus fully understood the problem. From the first words and actions of
his public ministry on earth as the Messiah through his final instructions to
his disciples before he returned to the heavenly realm, he was constantly describing, explaining, and demonstrating the reality of the Kingdom. With
direct statements and instructions and with parables he tried to help people
understand it and want to be part of it under his reign.

When the disciples asked about their positions in the coming kingdom, he explained that in his kingdom organization people would follow
and lead each other as humble servants, not as power-wielding, self-serving
leaders like those who control the "normal" organizations of this world. He
explained that he would suffer and die so they and all others could join his
Kingdom and seek to extend the experience of the Kingdom as broadly as
possible on earth.

Despite all Jesus' repeated explanations to his disciples, his Kingdom
was still invisible, incomprehensible, and not real for them until he rose
from death and returned to explain it all again, one last time. "He talked
to them about the Kingdom of God" (Acts 1:3). He declared himself to be
the Savior of the world, the one and only person through whom your sins
can be forgiven, and you can be reconciled to God, fit for eternal life with
God, and accepted as a citizen of the Kingdom of God. He also declared
himself to be the ultimate ruler with "complete authority" over everything
and everyone "in heaven and on earth" (Matt. 28:18-19).

He explained that his Kingdom is "already, but not yet." It already exists and is advancing, but it is not yet physically apparent with dominion
over all people and all of creation. It is near and all around, and it is a living
spiritual presence within each believer, but it is not empirically evident.
So, he sent them out to tell everyone everywhere to believe in and follow a
divine King who had come to earth in human form, then left earth and is
now temporarily absent from sight here on earth, but he is physically real,
spiritually present, and living in each of his followers now. He will someday
return to earth to reign over one unified and eternal Kingdom of a New
Heaven and Earth. Simply, but miraculously, by sincerely believing that it is
true, any person would be spiritually reborn as a new and different person
who would be part of God's Kingdom in this life and experience eternal life
with God in the life to come after death in this earthly realm. Though it

seemed logically impossible, Jesus Christ the King promised that his Holy Spirit would be his life in every such believing follower. His Spirit would guide them into God's truth and give them the power they would need to live in the present earthly life and forever after as children of the heavenly Father and citizens of the Kingdom of God.

While King Jesus was visibly present on earth, he gave his followers a core purpose and guiding principles for their actions. They should tell everyone on earth the Good News about Jesus Christ, the savior and king of the world, and encourage people to believe this truth and become new persons in Christ's kingdom. Every follower of Christ should make the very real but temporarily invisible Kingdom of Christ their guiding example and first concern in every aspect of their life. They should pray and work for God's kingdom to come on earth now as it already is in heaven, including all their servant-leadership and servant-followership. They should love and care about their neighbors as they do themselves, blessing as many people as possible in all their varied organizations in the earthly realm.

Organizations are essential in the joy of understanding, experiencing, and sharing the greatness of the Kingdom of God.

Jesus Christ, the "visible image of the invisible God" (Colossians 1:15), came from the heavenly realm of God's Kingdom to the earthly realm of the Kingdom in human form. He joyfully called himself the Son of Man, the Son of God, and the Christ/the Messiah. He came to announce, describe, and explain the Kingdom of God; to present himself as its King; and to invite every person to be forgiven of their sinful rejection of God by believing in Jesus as Savior and being reconciled to God.

Before God's Kingdom becomes the visible reign of power and glory over all the earth, the divine Kingdom advances from the heavenly realm into the earthly realm as an invisible spiritual presence and power within those persons who accept Jesus Christ as their Savior and sovereign King. Jesus presented himself as that King and demonstrated his sovereign authority and power with miracles and an explanatory message. He called people to repent of their sin and accept God's forgiveness and salvation by faith in him, and he invited those who believe in him to become his followers in his Kingdom. He gave extensive instructions about how to live as faithful, wise, and effective kingdom citizens now on the earth, with confident faith in the future fulfilment of God's great kingdom plan.

As recorded in the four gospel accounts, Jesus came to the earthly realm the first time in humility as teacher, example, and sacrificial Savior. His return will be with sovereign power when he will vanquish Satan, eliminate all evil, and make all things right, fully establishing his perfect and eternal rule over every person, every organization, and all creation on a cleansed and renewed earth. In addition to giving his followers many illustrative parables and specific instructions, Jesus also gave comprehensive core directives to guide their actions in every possible situation during the present period when he is physically absent from the earthly realm.

At the beginning of his public ministry in what is commonly known as the Sermon on the Mount, Jesus said: "Seek the Kingdom of God above all else, and live righteously, and he [your Father in heaven] will give you everything you need" (Matthew 6:33). Later, as his small band of specially chosen followers matured, Jesus sent them out to spread the kingdom news to "the people of Israel—God's lost sheep. Go and announce to them that the Kingdom of Heaven is near" (Matthew 10:5-7).

As he ended his time on earth as servant and savior, Jesus met the eleven disciples in Galilee and said: "I have been given all authority in heaven and on earth. Therefore, go and make disciples of all the nations, baptizing them in the name of the Father and Son and the Holy Spirit. Teach these new disciples to obey all the commands I have given you. And be sure of this: I am with you always, even to the end of the age" (Matthew 28:18-20).

The kingdom vision includes the initial promise to Abraham; the experience of the people of Israel before the coming of Jesus Christ; the earthly life, teaching, death, and resurrection of Jesus; and the present reality of followers of Jesus in the age of the Church. The gloriously visible manifestation of the unified Kingdom will come on earth as it is in heaven under the reign of Christ the King when he visibly returns to earth with power and glory. God "will bring everything together under the authority of Christ— everything in heaven and on earth" (Ephesians 1:10). Everything includes every organization.

The Kingdom of God on earth advances now one human decision at a time. And it also comes as the inscrutable plan of God moves in human affairs and in the events of nature toward his ultimate purpose in a unified earth and heaven. The Kingdom of God is a visible reality now in the heavenly realm. On earth now it is normally invisible to humans, with one notable exception: the earthly activity and, on rare occasions, the earthly visibility of angels from the heavenly realm. The Kingdom is present now whenever and wherever the reign of Christ is accepted, and most significantly in the life of any believing follower and in the life of the Church. "The Kingdom of God can't be detected by visible signs [now on earth] . . . [but] the Kingdom of God is already among you" (Luke 17:20-21 NLT).

The vision includes your personal decisions and actions and the policies, practices, cultures, and outcomes of every organization you are part of. There is no complete and perfect list of all those desired conditions, but the following list provides a suggestive place to start as you move toward the Kingdom ideal.

What life is like now in the heavenly realm of the Kingdom is what you can pray and work for in the present earthly realm, in every organization and every relationship.

Consistency—faithful predictability that allows people to safely plan and act

Dignity—respect for the worth of every person as made in God's image

Effectiveness—followership and leadership that advances the Kingdom ideal

Empathy—authentic recognition of feelings, fears, needs, and hopes

Ethics—behavior and treatment of people that is right in a given context

Faithfulness—loyal commitment to Christ and the welfare of all people

Fulfillment—satisfaction of becoming the person God created you to be

Generosity—that overcomes selfish greed and moves "from mine to ours"

Gentleness—the least painful and damaging way to do or say something

Goodness—Godlike actions; wanting or doing what God approves

Grace—action that tempers justice with unmerited compassion and redemption

Health—all dimensions of physical, emotional, relational, and spiritual well being

Hope – expectation that a desired condition is possible

Humility—admission of ignorance or incapacity that allows learning and growth

Integrity—being what you claim to be and doing what you say you will do

Joy—positive emotion that is deeper and more enduring than happiness

Justice—fair, equal, proportionate, and appropriate treatment of every person

Kindness—thoughtful consideration of others beyond basic norms

Love—strong positive feelings, approval, and/or caring for a person

Mercy—justified leniency with recognition that actions have consequences

Morality—behavior and treatment of people that is right and good in the absolute

Patience—allowance of time and support to correct mistakes or failures

Peace—Shalom of wholeness, safety, and well-being in healthy relationships

Self-control—respect for appropriate boundaries of behavior

Stewardship—earthly ownership now is practiced as kingdom-first stewardship

Truth—full factual honesty that is not misleading or incomplete

Meditation

> During the 40 days after his crucifixion, he appeared to the apostles from time to time, and he proved to them in many ways that he was actually alive. And he talked to them about the Kingdom of God. . . . So when the apostles were with Jesus, they kept asking him, "Lord, has the time come for you to free Israel and restore our kingdom?"
>
> He replied, "The Father alone has the authority to set those dates and times, and they are not for you to know. But you will receive power when the Holy Spirit comes upon you. And you will be my witnesses, telling people about me everywhere . . . to the ends of the earth."
>
> After saying this, he was taken up into a cloud while they were watching, and they could no longer see him. (Acts 1:3-9)

Like Jesus' followers when he lived on earth as Son of Man and Son of God Messiah, our first inclination is to want God to establish our kingdom—our family, our church, and our other organizations. They wanted to know when Jesus was going to give Israel their own king again so that they could be powerful and successful above the other nations of this world. But that vision was too small, so one last time Jesus explained that their assignment was to go to the ends of the earth telling all people everywhere about Jesus Christ and his one true Kingdom.

Then he did the most compelling thing possible to ensure that they would understand the greatness of his Kingdom. He left them! He floated away from them into a cloud and disappeared. The one person who could make the kingdom a reality was gone. Without a king who was physically present and visible there could be no physically visible kingdom. And yet the instructions of King Jesus were clear and simple. Everywhere you go, in every relationship, every situation, and every organization, by faith in the power of the Holy Spirit, make the Kingdom of Christ your first concern and invite everyone to worship the King and join his Kingdom.

Talking with God

You could have stayed, Jesus. You could have swept away every puny bit of resistance and established your kingdom on earth right then. But obviously, that was not your plan. Your plan included millions of others and me to whom you gave the opportunity to freely choose you and your kingdom by faith instead of taking one of the other options with their compellingly visible attractions and obvious immediate benefits here and now.

You are the suffering Savior and self-sacrificing King of love and light, of forgiveness and freedom. You do not coerce me to trust you. Instead, you silently forgive me and die in my place so that I can freely choose your kingdom of peace and eternal life with you. I am overwhelmed with gratitude, my Savior, my King, my God. Help me know you and follow you better. And teach me how to know whom to follow in this life and how to support their leadership to advance your Kingdom. Amen.

Questions and Issues

A. How do you reconcile Jesus' instruction—to not worry about your earthly responsibility to feed and clothe yourself and your family—with his instruction to always make the heavenly Kingdom of God your top priority?

B. What are some practical examples of making the Kingdom of God your highest priority in your family life? When you vote? On Facebook or LinkedIn?

C. What are some practical examples of making the Kingdom of God your highest priority in your work life, especially if you work for a secular organization, when you consider that Jesus said his Kingdom is not an earthly kingdom and not of this world? How does an unearthly kingdom relate to your duty to make a living?

The Visible Organization That Advances the Invisible Kingdom

The Kingdom of God is a unique organization with two realms: heaven and earth. The heavenly realm includes angels who sometimes become visible on earth, as the Bible describes in various accounts in both Old and New Testaments, and as some people report personal experience. In his glorified body after his resurrection Jesus moved between the two realms, being instantly visible or invisible to humans on earth. Since his physical departure from earth, his followers have his (invisible) Holy Spirit alive in them, but the King and his Kingdom continue to be invisible.

Immediately after Jesus Christ ascended out of the earthly realm, the apostles began to create the visible organization that would carry out their kingdom-building mandate. They organized the Church as the visible body of Christ on earth till he returns with power and glory to establish his unified Kingdom of Heaven and Earth. At the first "church business meeting," they chose a person to replace Judas on the leadership team. They organized regular meetings for prayer and for discussion to ensure clarity and consensus about the huge assignment Jesus had given them. Seven weeks after Jesus' resurrection the believers were meeting together when the promised Holy Spirit came upon all those who were assembled and waiting. Peter had been anointed to give the message to an audience that God had gathered from the nations, cultures, and languages of the world, including non-Jewish Gentiles.

The new organization grew rapidly. Three thousand people "believed what Peter said (and) were baptized and added to the church. . . . They joined with the other believers and devoted themselves to the apostles' teaching and fellowship, sharing in the Lord's supper and in prayer" (Acts 2:41-42). All the believers had regular meetings where they joyfully agreed to the core value of generously sharing all the resources they could assemble with those who needed it most.

From its very beginning, the Church has been a unique organization in and for the Kingdom of Jesus Christ. If you are a Christ-follower, the Church is a visible and essential organization in your life, because it serves and seeks to advance the Kingdom of Christ. Your local church congregation is a visible group of people and the physical location where the group gathers is also visible. The massive super-organization of all Christ's followers everywhere on earth is a visible reality, including all its church-related schools, clinics, missions, relief agencies, Bible-translators, and hundreds of other kinds of suborganizations. The priority you give to the health and effectiveness of the Church helps ensure that every part of the Church seeks first the Kingdom of God in every decision, policy, plan, and program.

The Church is a very complex and elaborately structured global organization, with countless suborganizations that contribute a wide variety of distinctive identities, titles, roles, corporate forms, organizational cultures, and missional purposes. The Church has a unique role in advancing the Kingdom and it must adapt to thousands of cultures, languages, and governmental conditions. The Church is obvious and empirically present as a kingdom organization on earth in a way that is not yet true of the Kingdom of God in the earthly realm.

The Church—local and worldwide and taken as a whole—is a unique organization guided and empowered by the Holy Spirit to advance the Kingdom of God. In addition to being an organization, the Church also has other identities that include being the organic living body of Christ on earth during his physical absence and being the bride of Christ. The Church is also a unique *polis,* a political organization with certain forms of temporal influence that derive in part from its role as the body of Christ in his absence, from the moral authority created by its special mission and magnitude worldwide.

However, the Church is not called or authorized by Jesus Christ to use or even co-opt temporal power the way other organizations do for their protection or to attempt to enforce certain behaviors or conditions. The Church has fallen into that trap many times in its 2100-year history. Individual Christians do answer when God calls them to serve him in government, from local to international agencies, and those Jesus-followers can bear witness to God's kingdom ideals for society and help guide government actions toward the values and character of the Kingdom with wise laws and effective programs that seek to fulfil the role of government as ordained by God.

Follower Case: I Don't Follow Them

During a break in a seminar on leading and following that I was facilitating with a group of pastors and other church leaders, one of the senior pastors loudly declared that I was simply wrong to suggest that he needed to be a more effective follower or intentionally develop the skills and habits of engaged followership. He made sure that I and everyone nearby knew that God had called him to pastoral leadership, and he had been trained for leadership, not followership. The members of his congregation were the sheep who followed him. He was their spiritual leader, and they were instructed by scripture to do what he told them to do (Hebrews 13:17). Their job was to obey and support him as their spiritual leader. "I don't follow them. They follow me. And we are all following Christ." He believed that the Church as a whole needed more agreeable, obedient, and hard-working followers who listened to their pastor, trusted his guidance, and acted on it.

A local church, as well as a larger denominational church body, can mistakenly, and sometimes inadvertently, adopt some version of the leader-centric, power-based paradigm of the world in which its members live and work. The congregational leaders may replace the authentically reciprocal followership and leadership with executives who lead with power but who do not listen to, learn from, or practice accountability with their congregation. Partly because the Church is so obvious as a global, multicultural organization with visible identity and influence in the world, it is easy for a congregational church to look and operate so much like the surrounding world that it lessens or loses its distinctive identity, character, mission, vision, and values. And it can lose the model of following and leading as equally important interdependent roles.

The leader-centric pastor who rejected my premise seemed threatened by the prospect of having strong, actively engaged followers. In order to "be large and in charge," he was willing to operate without the corporate wisdom, power, and support of the Church as a dynamic community of partners in ministry who are guided and gifted by God's Spirit. When the seminar resumed, my brief and guarded comment was that they would not be able to evaluate him, hold him accountable, inform him, or truly love and care for him. And that one measure of his model of leadership would appear when his followers had to choose his successor.

The Church is the visible agent and model of the Kingdom, The Kingdom of Jesus Christ is a true kingdom that fully satisfies the basic definition of a real organization with many suborganizations. The Kingdom is a group of people identified and unified by a shared interest and purpose. Citizens of the Kingdom of God have a shared commitment of loyalty to Jesus Christ, their one true leader, who calls them to a concomitant commitment to the welfare of all the other members and potential members of the Kingdom.

The Kingdom of Jesus Christ is a spiritual, sociocultural, physical, economic, political, temporal, and eternal reality. It exists now in the heavenly realm, and it is in the process of coming on earth as it is in heaven. The Kingdom is real within every person who welcomes the sovereign reign of Christ the King, and it is also real in every element of the entire natural creation that awaits its redemption from the effects of sin. But as an organization, you cannot physically see it yet. The Kingdom comes into existence spiritually when a person stops trying to save and lead themselves and accepts Jesus as their Savior and King. The presence of the invisible Kingdom can be inferred from the actions of its citizens who seek to make the Kingdom their highest priority as the Church and in all of life.

Meditation

Christ is the visible image of the invisible God. He existed before God made anything at all and is supreme over all creation. Christ is the one through whom God created everything in heaven and earth. He made the things we can see and the things we can't see—kings, kingdoms, rulers, and authorities.

. . . Christ is the head of the church, which is his body. (Colossians 1:15-18 NLT)

You can see a king, a visible person, and the various representatives of that government with authority to act. But a kingdom is basically a mental construct. God is invisible. Jesus Christ is the physical, visible image of the invisible God. Everything that humans know and experience as reality is the creation-work of Jesus Christ. That creation includes visible organizational realities like the Church and presently invisible realities like the Kingdom. When Jesus came to earth as a human, he made pure spirit and energy tangible and visible to humans. He inaugurated his Kingdom and began the process by which all creatures and all organizations would eventually become clearly and gloriously subordinate to his perfect rule in his Kingdom. It begins with accepting by faith the reality and priority of an invisible heavenly realm of spiritual reality.

Before the Church existed, and above and beyond the Church while it now exists, and after the Church is no longer, the ultimate purpose and primary concern of every person in the very organization should be the Kingdom of God under the reign of Christ.

Talking with God

Heavenly Father, help me understand and accept by faith the reality that I cannot see or fully understand. You alone are the one true God: eternal, immortal, invisible, all-knowing, pure spirit, and the essence of all energy. You are light and truth and love. In and through Jesus Christ you have made invisible spirit and invisible energy become visible in the creation that we experience as space and time and physical objects over which Christ rules supreme.

All creation brings you glory, and part of that glory is the freedom you give us to trust you; to choose Christ as our King; to choose above all else your Kingdom that is invisible now; and to choose your way of salvation, your truth, and your life as the body of Christ now in the visible Church. Help me accept what I see so dimly and understand so imperfectly. Help me see by faith so that I may more fully worship you with grateful joy.

Jesus, you must bring in your Kingdom. But while the Heavenly Father in patient grace waits for the perfect moment of that fulfillment, help us understand and respond to your call for every person to honor and worship you now by constantly moving individually and as organizations toward the beauty and glory of your Kingdom. While we are waiting and working, we ask for your Kingdom to come in us. Amen.

Questions and Issues

A. Jesus told his twelve specially chosen disciples that he had been given "all authority in heaven and on earth." Why don't the gospels say anywhere that Jesus prepared them to lead the kingdom effort with authority that he delegated to them? Why did he tell them to serve and teach instead of seeking power as political leaders?

B. Jesus said, "My Kingdom is not an earthly kingdom. . . . My kingdom is not of this world" (John 18:36). How can you make his invisible and nonearthly Kingdom your highest priority in all the earthly organizations that you engage with daily for almost everything you need to sustain physical life?

Visible and Invisible Organizational Realities

T he visible organizational arrangement of formal positions, power, rewards, policies, professed values, and actual behavioral patterns provide the obvious and usual way to understand an organization. The formal structures and systems of leadership and management, organizational charts, compensation policies, market position, financial strength, and employee morale of an organization are commonly understood and are discussed with common language.

What must be learned and practiced is seeing what is not so obvious, the elements that are sometimes actually invisible to the person who has not learned to see organizations with a different framework. Leadership is inherently visible in most organizations, and leaders are readily identifiable. Followership is typically invisible and followers are usually treated as incidental byproducts of leadership. Getting different results begins with seeing and doing things differently. The key is seeing what would normally not be obvious to you, and possibly not even visible. It is part of the reality of an organization, but it is not obvious and thus it becomes invisible and irrelevant. But it is still there and it matters, and seeing it allows you to understand the organizational situation differently and get better outcomes.

In the earthly realm, the Church is a visible organization and the Kingdom of God is invisible. Through Christ "God created everything in heaven and earth. He made the things we can see and the things we can't see—kings, kingdoms, rulers, and authorities" (Colossians 1:16 NLT). God's original creation included creating organizations. A king or other kind of political ruler is a visible reality. A ruler's authority is an invisible reality. God made both. You can physically see the king that God made. God also made the kingdom or nation that is governed, but it is an invisible reality that exists in the minds of those who recognize the ruler's invisible but very real authority under God's ultimate sovereignty. "Christ is the visible image of the invisible God. He existed before God made anything at all and is supreme over all creation" (Colossians 1:15 NLT).

The Kingdom of God is a real kingdom that fully satisfies the basic definition of an organization. The Kingdom of Jesus Christ exists wherever the sovereign authority of King Jesus is recognized with effect. It includes all his creation and specifically his angels and all the humans who worship and follow him as their leader. His followers are unified by a shared interest, purpose, and commitment of loyalty to Jesus Christ, their one true leader, who calls them to a concomitant commitment to the welfare of all the other members and potential members of his organization.

Before the Church existed, and above and beyond the Church while it now exists, and when the Church as a distinct and separate organization no longer exists, the ultimate purpose and primary concern of every person in every organization should be the Kingdom of God under the reign of Christ. When Jesus came to earth, he made the invisible God visible; he made pure spirit and energy tangible in human form; he personally inaugurated his Kingdom and began the culminating phase of the process by which all creatures and all organizations would eventually become clearly and gloriously subordinate to his perfect rule in his perfect and eternal Kingdom. Jesus' teaching about his Kingdom and his identity as Savior and King was clear, simple, and all inclusive.

Your Father will give you everything you need to flourish from day to day if you "make the Kingdom of God your primary concern. So don't be afraid, little flock. For it gives your Father great happiness to give you the Kingdom" (Luke 12:31-32 NLT). When Jesus spoke these words, the organized Church did not yet exist, so there was no way to describe and explain how the Church would be the most visible and recognizable organizational manifestation of the Kingdom of God for thousands of years. But before the Church existed, and above and beyond the Church while it now exists, and after the Church no longer exists, the ultimate purpose and primary concern of every person and of every organization should be the Kingdom of God under the reign of Christ the King.

The Heavenly Father is delighted to give his children all the benefits of membership in his Kingdom with one comprehensive guiding principle. In every situation, in every organization, in every relationship, in everything you say and do, "make the Kingdom of God your primary concern." Let everything be measured by this one standard. Jesus does not expect his followers to achieve perfection in conformity with God's will in order to be part of his Kingdom. He simply says to make it your top priority. Let nothing else be more important to you in any decision or action. He knows that you will do it imperfectly. All he asks is that you truly and consistently want it, desire it, passionately and purely long and pray and work for it.

Because even pure and simple wanting is not possible to fully achieve, and because the Kingdom is spiritual and within you as well as physical and beyond you to the farthest speck of matter in the universe, Jesus Christ the King must bring in his kingdom. So, while God in patient grace waits for the perfect moment, the King calls every person to honor and worship him now by constantly moving as individuals and as organizations toward the ideal of the only perfect organization, his Kingdom.

Thus, when Jesus taught his followers how to pray, he instructed them to ask God to establish his physical visible Kingdom as soon as possible. They were to pray for it. And praying for something requires the petitioner to do anything logically possible to express that prayer in action. Praying for God's Kingdom to come means acting so that every person and every organization would be increasingly aligned with the glorious and joyous perfection of Christ and his Kingdom, the one perfect organization of devoted followers under the one perfect leader.

Meditation

> May your kingdom come soon. May your will be done here on earth [not] just as it [already] is in heaven. (Matthew 6:10)

By giving his followers explicit authority and guidance to pray for God's Kingdom to come and for God's eternal plan to be fully accomplished on earth right now, Jesus provided the logical framework for knowing and doing what really matters most in every human decision, emotion, desire, relationship, organization, and social system. Prayers and actions must reinforce each other without any overt or covert contradiction. When you pray about something you commit yourself to align your thoughts, feelings, and actions with whatever God wants to accomplish in relationship to that prayer.

You do not pray to align God with what you want but rather to align yourself and everyone and everything else on earth with what God wants, with God's ultimate plan to redeem the whole creation. When you pray for the complete realization of the absolute reign of Christ, you also are committing yourself to work to see the Kingdom and to advance it in any way you can.

Talking with God

Almighty God, praying for your Kingdom to come soon, to become reality here and now, obviously threatens our current reality. It alters what we look for and what we really see in the world around us. Nothing is the same. Nothing means what it normally means in the fallen and distorted condition of things. It is a revolution that attracts me, but it also frightens me if I forget, even for a moment, that Jesus reassures all of us that we do not need to worry about anything. It makes no logical sense to pray and worry.

So, help me pray with eager anticipation. Help me recognize what you are up to and joyfully join in. When I cannot comprehend what you are doing, fill me with your "peace which is far more wonderful than the human mind can understand" (Phil 4:7 NLT). Fill me with your peace because you are not only the frightening, righteous, almighty God, you are also my loving heavenly Father who sent your son to redeem us from our human rebellion and prepare us for your New Heaven and your New Earth. Give me eyes of faith to see what is otherwise invisible, to see the greatness of your Kingdom and the splendor of my King. By faith I thank you. Amen.

Questions and Issues

A. How does praying for the Kingdom of God to come affect your feelings, desires, values, relationships, and behavior?

B. When you pray for God's will to be done on earth as it is in heaven, are you expecting to see or experience something different now on earth, or are you praying for Jesus Christ to return as soon as possible to visibly reign over a unified Kingdom of Heaven and Earth?

CHAPTER 8

You Believe in Leadership because You Can See It

Seeing is believing. You may not completely trust any particular leader in every situation, but most people believe in the reality and importance of leaders and leadership, even though neither the leadership literature nor common usage agree on a working definition of leadership, or even on who is or is not an effective leader. Bernard Bass identifies and develops hundreds of concepts, definitions, analytical frameworks, operational approaches, typologies, taxonomies, classifications, theories, styles, patterns, and models of leadership.[4] Joseph Rost identified 221 different definitions of leadership that he found in 587 books, book chapters, and journal articles that had the word leadership in the title, starting in the 1920s when the earliest such books appeared.[5] Just as enlightening is the fact that the other 366 sources that Rost found on leadership explored the subject of leadership without even trying to define it.

That lack of a uniform understanding is why every leadership article, video, training manual, or book provides its own working definition of leadership that the author will use, or else leaves it undefined. Despite the lack of a consensus definition of exactly what leadership is or even what it looks like in practice, most people believe in it anyway, whatever it is. You can believe in leadership even when you have lost trust in any particular leader because you can see it. You can believe in the notion of leadership even if you do not understand it the same way as others. You can believe in the premise of leadership even when you do not get your desired outcomes. You believe in leadership because you and everyone else can see it. You can see the power of a person in a position of formal organizational leadership or in an informal role that changes minds and hearts.

But the power of followership is typically invisible also and thus naturally seems inconsequential unless there is a large-scale expression of disloyalty of some kind, such as a work stoppage, a mass protest, or other form of revolt. Otherwise, followership in the dominant culture naturally is treated as a passive factor rather than an active force, a result rather than a cause. A leader has power as an individual. Except in unusual circumstances, followers only have power when they combine forces and act together, and leaders typically do not welcome such events.

An organizational model sometimes called collaborative leadership implicitly recognizes followership, but the title overtly asserts that it is about more inclusive leadership, not about more powerful followership. It can be a way for followers to feel like leaders, or to influence leaders, or even coerce leaders. It can be a mechanism to advance goodwill or good feelings because the insights of followers have at least been heard in the process of making decisions that affect them. In some cases, it can improve organizational harmony, wisdom, and success. But all such arrangements are still a different matter from the pattern of mutual influence that results from recognizing role and function distinctions between powerful following and powerful leading where those involved fill either role as needed, and all participants are competent and humble enough to listen and learn. Each depends on the other, but the primal power resides in and springs from effective followership. It is not a case of organizational alchemy that makes following invisible. Rather, leadership positions, power, and functions are visible. Followership is supportive and dispersed and not easily recognized for its collective effect that identifies the leaders whom the followers are willing to make successful. Wise and effective followers know that wise and effective leadership is always needed to produce the ongoing change that benefits all organizational stakeholders.

Given hundreds of concepts of leadership and few if any working definitions of followership, there is one elegantly simple concept proposed by Peter Drucker and others that provides a consistent platform for all the varieties and concepts of leadership. It is useful because it is essentially a truism that is logically impossible to contradict when two terms mutually define each other.

A leader has followers, and a follower has a leader.

If leadership exists in any situation, then followership of some kind must coexist with it. Where followership exists, there must be leadership of some kind. It is logically and practically impossible to have either one without the other. One humorous description puts it this way: If no one is following, you are not leading; you are just taking a walk by yourself.

The simplest and most basic element that creates the leading-following phenomenon in every situation is *influence*. For any leadership to happen, someone in a leadership role must have some form of influence in the experience of someone in a follower role who trusts that influence to some degree. Whoever has such influence has a leadership role, even if such a de facto leader does not acknowledge or accept it.

The leading-following phenomenon exists whenever someone accepts another person's influence.

A ready example of this concept is apparent in the social media platforms that explicitly provide for this reality by allowing a person to become a "follower" of some remote person whom they experience via audio and/or video. The system identifies the leader of such followers as an "influencer." The system does not require any real interpersonal relationship, and the identities often do not exist in the context of any purposeful organization. But the existence of influence creates a leader-follower dyad.

When you are convinced that strong leadership is the primary and singularly critical key to a healthy and successful organization, you pay attention to leadership, whether you are leading or following. You develop, honor, evaluate, and reward leadership. You give leadership credit when things go well, and you modify your followership commitment if things go badly.

But in order to maintain an exclusive preoccupation with leadership, you naturally and consistently tend to ignore the fact that effective leading only exists if there is effective following, and you typically but erroneously tend to assume that leaders create their followers. You take followership as a given, something that just happens if you have leadership. You may study, teach, read about, and subsidize leadership development but still ignore followership development, and you assume that the followership just happens somehow if you have the right leadership and organizational structure.

In the end, you pay a high price for such ignorance of followership in the form of unhealthy, ineffective, and too often ultimately toxic organizations that do not serve people well. Not recognizing, valuing, and developing followership easily and often renders the organization unable to attract or support the leadership that they must have to achieve the necessary organizational success. That is how the transaction works with this world's predilection for powerful leadership and obedient or passive followership that is usually invisible and not valued. But Jesus said that his Kingdom on earth is different.

Follower Case: My son will be their leader.

On the last day of the school year, a mother was picking up her son from the preschool childcare at her church. She explained to the staff that the boy would continue attending at that same level for another year, despite his being normal age and development. She was holding him back so he could start Kindergarten a year later and be a year older than the others in his class from then on through school. She stated her rationale with brazen simplicity. "I want him to be a leader, not a follower." What she really meant was, "When they all grow up, I want my son to be the respected, important, well-paid, powerful boss over these other kids. He will be their leader and tell them what to do, and they will be his followers."

This woman was confident that she was just doing what was best for her son, but unwittingly she exemplified the selective blindness that distorts our values and shared vision of reality. There is a more complete and accurate vision of reality that values her son as a follower just as much as a leader, and that allows him to become more effective in both roles, not only at work but also in his family and in every role he will fill in all the varied kinds of social groups and systems in which he will function.

Meditation

Then the mother of James and John, the sons of Zebedee, came to Jesus with her sons. She knelt respectfully to ask a favor. "What is your request?" he asked.

She replied, "In your Kingdom, please let my two sons sit in places of honor next to you, one on your right and the other on your left." . . .

43

When the ten other disciples heard what James and John had asked, they were indignant. But Jesus called them together and said, "You know that the rulers in this world lord it over their people, and officials flaunt their authority over those under them. But among you it will be different. Whoever wants to be a leader among you must be your servant, and whoever wants to be first among you must become your slave." (Matthew 20:20-27)

In the world where Jesus lived and taught and announced his kingdom, a slave was the bottom of the socio-economic hierarchy. Some slaves were trusted to be servants and even stewards in a household, but the difference and distance between servants and masters was clear and firm. The role of slaves and servants is to follow the orders of their master for the pleasure and benefit of the master. Jesus does not invert this relationship but merges the two roles of servant and master in a new reality.

In the servant-leader role you exercise the prerogatives and powers of that role in other-serving for the welfare of the followers, not in self-serving for your own welfare at their expense. In the time that Jesus Christ was on earth, some servants had defined authority over other servants and even over the children of the master. If you want followers to serve your personal needs and satisfy your desires, you are simply a customer being served, not a leader who serves your followers by doing the work of leading.

As a servant-leader, you lead seeking what is good for others, not primarily for your own advantage. You give as a recipient. You lead with the mindset, heart intentions, and confident humility of a wise and effective follower. To be able to lead or follow as a wise servant, you must practice wise self-care and also humbly accept the physical, emotional, and spiritual care of others.

Talking with God

Almighty God, my loving father, I welcome your Holy Spirit to teach me how to see followership just as vividly and automatically as I see leadership. Not just the loud, angry following that demands the leaders do what the followers want for themselves. I want to see and practice wise, gracious, and highly effective following that skillfully sees and does what advances your Kingdom.

I want to habitually notice the sincere and effective following that truly helps the leadership succeed for the good of everyone. I want to see the work of following that is practiced by people in positions of leadership, and I want to recognize, encourage, honor, and practice the power of wise and effective followership that produces successful leadership for your Kingdom. Amen.

Questions and Issues

A. How do you evaluate the decision and rationale of the mother in the follower case? Was she correct in her assessment of the situation and was her decision justified?

B. In what ways was the mother in the follower case thinking and acting like the mother of James and John when she asked Jesus to favor her sons, and are there any differences?

C. When Jesus responded to the request of James and John and their mother, what principles was he applying regarding a kingdom perspective on leadership and followership? Is it wrong for a person to feel that they should be leading in a particular situation? Is it right to ask God to allow you to have a certain leadership position or role?

D. How do you usually decide whose influence to accept and thus have a leadership role in your life? What principles or situational factors affect your leadership choices?

Following and Leading in the Cosmic Conflict

J esus invites every person to follow him, to make him the king of their life, accept his guidance, and seek to become more like him. Over time, committed followers increasingly think and act like their leader; an organization tends to "look like" the leader. The process is personal and individual, and it is also relational and organizational. As an individual, you are called to become more like Jesus. As a member of any organization, you are called to move your organizations to become more like the perfect organizational model of his Kingdom.

Jesus is the personal ideal. His Kingdom is the organizational ideal.

In the final fullness of the Kingdom of God, every organization will be a kingdom organization, operating on kingdom values and serving only the purposes of the King. He will rule over all the kingdoms of earth, over every organization great and small. Until that kingdom age begins and the earthly and heavenly realms are one under his perfect rule, the Kingdom of God clearly is not the primary concern of most individuals or of most organizations. Nevertheless, both the kingdom assignment and the corresponding kingdom prayer that Christ has given his followers still hold true. The challenge of advancing the kingdom—to say nothing of completing the kingdom—is humanly impossible to achieve, but the ultimate goal is clear and enduring, and with God and in God's timing, all things are possible.

The obvious problem is that the whole creation, including every person and every organization, is innately flawed as part of the fallen imperfection of all creation. The natural world is part of the Kingdom; it is wondrous but also marred and fallen. Humans are constantly tempted to give first priority to someone other than Jesus Christ and to something other than his Kingdom. Most often they choose themselves. Even churches and the organizations of Christendom too often succumb to the temptation of something other than his Kingdom.

Human imperfection in a disrupted natural order of all creation would be enough of a challenge by itself. But the situation is far more grave than the simple inability of people to live up to the perfect standard of God's Kingdom. The dark and stark reality is that the Kingdom of Jesus Christ is not the only supernatural kingdom in the cosmos. Satan and the kingdom of darkness that he rules with deception and pride are every bit as real as Christ and his Kingdom of Light, Truth, and Love. The evil hides, invisible in darkness and disguised by deceit. And because every person is bent and disoriented by sin toward self-centered pride, and the fallen world feels so threatening and dangerous, the strategy of the Great Deceiver is frighteningly effective.

The cosmic conflict between these two organizations and their leaders will continue until Jesus Christ returns visibly to earth. In the end, the Kingdom of Light prevails, the kingdom of darkness and its evil prince are destroyed, and Jesus Christ reigns supreme over all his creation. But until then you are given the opportunity to voluntarily choose Jesus Christ as your Savior and King and make his Kingdom your primary concern in every aspect of your personal and organizational life.

The cosmic conflict is the necessary concomitant of the divine cosmic conundrum. God wants you to freely choose to love him and serve him rather than yourself. But how can you be truly free to voluntarily choose to love and trust God if the alternative is his (righteous) condemnation and your death? That does not feel like a truly free choice of a trustworthy offer of sincere love.

God's solution to this conundrum is the suffering and death of his incarnate son Jesus on the cross. So, the choice you make is truly voluntary. You do not have to die, just as Jesus did not have to die. It is a real choice that must be made in faith that God has demonstrated that his love is true and trustworthy. In this time period after the suffering, death, resurrection, and departure of the King, he invites every person to choose to love, worship, and follow him and seek his Kingdom in every possible way.

Free will is the core principle. So just as you are free to choose or reject Jesus Christ as your king, if you do choose him, you are similarly free

47

to choose from among the countless strategies you may use to follow the King and advance his Kingdom organization. There is no one organizational or programmatic strategy that is always correct in every situation. You are granted freedom by the King to prayerfully, shrewdly, humbly, creatively, and confidently develop and implement personal and organizational strategies to advance the Kingdom in various situations. He did not mandate or limit your strategic or organizational creativity. You are expected to choose from the full range of strategies that align with the beliefs and values of his Kingdom.

However, values and core principles matter. Jesus warned his followers to not adopt the prideful values and coercive strategies of the dominant culture that ultimately benefit his enemy, Satan. Instead, Jesus calls you to follow and serve him by wisely choosing leaders who seek to effect kingdom values. And by logical extension, when followers call you to lead, you lead as their servant and for their benefit as you work together to seek first the Kingdom.

There is one simple fact of organizational reality that must inform all organizational life, especially if it exists to advance the Kingdom above all. Consistently respecting this core truism enables you to truly put God's Kingdom first in every organizational situation and achieve the highest form of organizational success that otherwise seems utterly unrealistic. Healthy organizations succeed at both parts of this principle.

In every organization everything is done by someone who is following or leading.

And often a person acts in both the leading and following roles simultaneously. The dominant culture is leader-centric and does not see or value the followership part of the organization or of your work.

When you make the Kingdom your model, leading and following are equally important and valued in every organization.

Both roles are to be filled with the heart of a servant. The kingdom perspective on organizations stands in sharp contrast to the typical organizational model where leading, and especially leading with power, is what really matters, and followers are treated as simply a passive byproduct of strong leadership. Instead, the responsibilities and competencies required of excellent and highly effective following must be intentionally developed.

The leadership role is learned. The followership role is also learned, and followership development must be an organizational priority just like leadership development has traditionally been. Every member of the organization must understand what effectiveness looks like in each role and value the contributions of each role.

Leadership development must include learning how to encourage, support, and engage full-spectrum followership, so that the organization benefits from the corporate wisdom of all members. Everyone must understand that loyalty as a follower includes ensuring that leaders know what they need to know to succeed and hold leadership accountable, just as leaders hold followers accountable.

The more you understand, value, develop, and implement the integration of these interdependent roles of following and leading in alignment with Jesus' teaching and example of mutual service, the organizational culture will contrast with the way these roles operate in the dominant culture that ultimately serves Satan's purposes. Doing the right thing can often feel risky when the competitor or regulator does not uphold righteous standards, but Jesus said that it is the path to have all your needs met.

Seeking first the Kingdom, doing the right thing, including valuing the servant-first mentality in both your following and your leading, will prosper the organization, whether or not people realize that it is more "like the kingdom." But you will see and rejoice when people and organizations wisely, effectively, and consistently live out the kingdom prayer and the kingdom-first assignment that Jesus gave all his followers. It feels risky to use such an alternate paradigm, but it offers a pathway to a kind of organizational success that otherwise remains unachievable.

Follower Case: Just a Follower

I am just a follower, not a leader. Everything we do here has to fit the system and standards and rules that corporate gives us. I know how everything works and I can do it all. If there are any questions or problems that I can't solve, the local owner, who's my boss, decides how to handle it. She is very nice to all us staff, and there's lots of stuff that I just do because I can see what is needed to serve our clients. I feel like she trusts me, especially in training the other staff or figuring out new procedures. And she usually likes my suggestions. Sometimes she needs to ask me about someone she doesn't know or something we do that she doesn't understand or wasn't aware of, but she is in charge and she is responsible for everything. I am very comfortable supporting her; I like my job and I feel good about how I do it. I have always just been a follower, not a leader.

In the Kingdom of God, no one is "just a follower." Everyone is first and always a follower, and everyone is responsible for following well. Sometimes, maybe even without realizing it, you are called to do the work of leading. Your ideal is to lead like Jesus led, as a servant. You lead with the humble learning heart and skills of an effective follower who wisely discerns who should lead and what support and guidance those leaders need from their followers to be successful. Edward Murphy summarizes it beautifully: Every leader needs "effective followers who can help overcome obstacles, resolve problems, and achieve the goals. . . . As an effective follower, your job is to make things happen for your boss."[6] Murphy provides a comprehensive and exquisitely practical manual for seeing and doing what your leader and your organization need to succeed, from an action plan to final evaluation and recording lessons learned. The specificity makes it obvious that effective followership is powerful!

Meditation

. . . your Father already knows your needs. He will give you all you need from day to day if you make the Kingdom of God your primary concern. So, don't be afraid, little flock. For it gives your Father great happiness to give you the Kingdom. (Luke 12:29-32 NLT)

The prince of darkness wants everyone to make some other kingdom or value-system or organization their primary concern. Anything but God's Kingdom! Just as happened with him, this evil prince wants the Godlikeness in each person to be distorted so that the primacy of the Kingdom of God will be replaced by the reign of the proud and rebellious creature instead of the Creator. Advancing your own kingdom seems very attractive and can even feel necessary, especially if your advancement seems closely linked to the advancement of God's Kingdom. Humanly speaking, the rationalization of such leading can seem fully justifiable.

Success in making "the Kingdom of God your primary concern" includes pursuing the vision of the Great Commission to "make disciples of all the nations." That kind of kingdom success requires eyes of faith and a grateful heart accepting a gift from the Creator and King who is coming back to earth to complete the redemption of the whole creation and inaugurate his glorious reign.

Talking with God

Heavenly Father, pride still preys on my most vulnerable point of weakness. My pride is so sneaky that I usually cannot even see it. Shine your light on the dark deception of my self-centered pride. Do whatever you need to do to ensure the humility that will allow me to learn and grow. I want to worship you and advance your Kingdom with everything I do.

I want to learn how to live more and more in the Kingdom of Light and always make the Kingdom of Jesus Christ my primary concern, in every relationship and every situation and decision, especially with my family, but also in my other relationships and my various organizations including my church congregation.

This ideal seems impossible. I cannot even consistently want it, let alone do it. But with you, every good and perfect gift is possible. With you, beauty and goodness become visible in the light of your perfect love. I want your Kingdom to come, starting in me and affecting every organization I am part of.

I admit I cannot do it. I don't even know what it looks like. But I trust you to shine your light and help me see it. Open my eyes. Show me your way. And give me the courage to act by faith on the clear call and instructions that my Savior and King, Jesus Christ, gave to all his followers. Thank you, Father. Thank you. Amen.

Questions and Issues

A. Why did God allow Lucifer to rebel and engage in cosmic conflict with him? Why did God allow a hoard of other angels to follow Lucifer and make him their leader in a power struggle against God on earth? Why does God value the option of rejecting him?

B. What can you learn for your own actions and interpersonal relationships from God's valuing of freedom of choice? Why is such personal freedom important enough to make all humans suffer the pain of a fallen and cursed earth?

C. As a follower choosing and supporting human leaders in the Church and other organizations, what are the implications, if any, of the normally invisible power of Satan's angels of darkness and deceit and the similarly invisible angels of light and truth?

D. What might you say to someone who says that they are "just a follower?"

Implications of Seeing What Is Not Obvious

C hrist is the visible image of the invisible God. Through Christ God created everything in the heavenly realms and on earth. He made the things we can see and the things we can't see—such as thrones and rulers (visible) and kingdoms and authorities (invisible) (Col. 1:15).

The things that you experience through the senses feel real, and you can assign them some level of relative importance in your life. What is "real and true" is limited to what the human senses can register and the human mind can record and organize. Intangible experiences like feelings, beliefs, values, hopes, and fears are objectified. Such invisible experiences become real, relevant, and important through the repetition of messages to the brain through the human senses. Countless communication channels—including both printed and electronic media—create reality with words and images and set priorities with repetition. Such messaging can make things feel "true" and important even if evidence and logic otherwise would render them probably untrue and/or relatively inconsequential. By contrast, a person, thing, or idea that is not made visible or sensorially present in the relevant culture normally tends to lose importance. Unless there is some effective counterinfluence, over time such invisible elements become irrelevant in a person's thinking and activities. Eventually, in practice, such things become not real. They do not exist. The logic is simple and culturally pervasive.

Out of sight, out of mind, out of existence.

Follower Case: We are mostly leaders, not followers

Albert was a successful pastor with the strengths of a person who is comfortable with innovative leadership in challenging circumstances. The Church had chosen him because they realized that they needed an unusual leader, and this man felt like the rare person who could lead them. He was impressed with the unusual breadth and depth of professional qualifications and leadership experience of the members, and with their energy, vision, knowledge of the Bible, strong financial and prayer support, and willingness to work.

During his candidacy, Albert affirmed their statement of faith including its emphasis on the church as the body of Christ, but he noted that he could not find statements in their documents about their particular identity, purposes, priorities, or distinctive programs. They said that was the kind of thing they expected him to help them develop. They wanted him to lead the church forward, including building consensus and action on such items.

Over time, as he learned their personal stories and their visions and ideas for a great church, he heard a consistent pattern. Most members had come from a frustrating or disappointing experience in their previous congregation. They were attracted to the spirit of freedom and innovation in this very dynamic congregation. But almost two years into his tenure as lead pastor, the church still had no actionable statements of a distinctive purpose or core values or priorities that he could help advance. Some great ideas, proposals, and draft documents had been considered, both for the church as a whole and for specific initiatives, and many people had offered to lead and/or to fund various efforts. But nothing ever moved past the early stages of a great idea. Strong people on the church board often could not reach consensus, and many items were rejected or deferred indefinitely.

In frustrated curiosity, the pastor tried an experiment. He chose one especially attractive proposal from a well-respected member, and he set out to personally recruit volunteers to join the effort. He asked each prospective participant if they thought it was a good idea and worth doing, and each prospect said that it was an excellent idea. When each person said they could not or would not commit to working on the project, he probed for a deeper understanding. After several tries one person explained what the pastor could not see, simply because it was missing: "I am basically a leader,

54

not a follower. So, I'm always looking for followers to help me do the things God puts on my heart. But I'm not looking for a leader who wants me to stop leading my team to help them succeed at their thing. I think there are a lot of us like me in this church. We are mostly leaders, not followers. I have to find my followers elsewhere."

Albert finally concluded that he was trying to lead a church full of strong leaders with few if any members who could or would follow and support him or anyone else in the church. They were enthusiastic Jesus-followers, but they could not justify diverting time and effort away from their own leadership calling and vision to support something or someone else. He realized that a church—like any other organization—where everyone is always and only a leader can unwittingly make most potential followers feel uncomfortable and unimportant. He viewed himself as a pastor who led from the pulpit, but who also valued ministry as a servant-follower, supporting and serving the members of the church in their needs and hopes. His experiment to lead a church of leaders did not go well. His efforts to develop "the heart and mind of a follower" produced no apparent response or results. He decided that they would never support him or each other as servant-followers, so he would never be able to be their pastoral servant-leader. He resigned.

If you cannot find any followers, do not bother looking for any leaders.

Meditation

At this point many of his disciples turned away and deserted him. Then Jesus turned to the Twelve and asked, "Are you also going to leave?"

Simon Peter replied, "Lord, to whom would we go? You have the words that give eternal life." (John 6:66-68)

The night before this great desertion by many of his disciples, the Twelve saw Jesus walk on the water and calm a frightening storm. Then while teaching in the synagogue of Capernaum, Jesus repeated four times that he was "the bread of life" that they needed to eat to be assured of eternal life. Most of them had eaten physical bread that Jesus had miraculously provided.

But they were unable to grasp that he was the spiritual bread of life, so they refused to continue following him and deserted. It is impossible to lead people who cannot see and accept the truth that defines the path forward to the desired condition, in this case, the path to eternal life.

Followership is an act of faith; you choose a leader you trust. Both elements are variable and invisible, but both are very real and each is a primal source of power for effective living in the present earthly realm of the Kingdom. Faith, hope, and love are enduring foundations of life now, but the greatest of these is love, for it will still exist in the heavenly Kingdom to come when faith and hope are no longer needed. And the organizations of that Kingdom will demonstrate effective following and leading made equally important and beautifully interdependent by the absence of sin and by the controlling centrality of love. That ideal guides relationships and organizations now as the people of God pray and work together as stewards in the Kingdom of God.

Talking with God

May your will be done and your Kingdom come on earth as it is in heaven. Help me sense the presence of your Spirit and see your kingdom wisdom in each of my relationships and organizations. Help me follow Jesus Christ my Savior and King as I choose and support the leaders we need. And if I need to do the work of leading, help me do it with the humble heart of a truly effective follower. Amen.

Questions and Issues

A. Followership and the Kingdom of God are invisible. What are other examples of invisible but important realities like electricity, justice, sound, gravity, prayer, and so forth? Jesus said that the communion elements should help his followers remember him until he visibly returns. What are some other potentially important realities that might fade?

B. How should you or your organization decide which invisible elements need to be maintained, cultivated, or referenced, and which can appropriately be released?

C. What are some ways to help remember and maintain the relevance of the personal and organizational invisible realities that need to be kept relevant?

D. What are some prayer reminders that work for you?

E. Jesus Christ is the head of the Church—his body on earth—and also King of the Kingdom of God, which makes both organizations totally leader-centric. Given that model, what, if anything, makes leader-centrism with passive followership problematic in churches and Christian organizations?

F. What, if anything, makes the invisible Kingdom of God real and relevant for you?

G. What are the theoretical or practical differences between working to advance your church or the global church, and working to advance the Kingdom of God?

H. Are there any exceptions to the general principle that everything in an organization is done by followers or leaders?

I. Are effective following and leading really equally important, or is one or the other more important in practice? Which one and why?

J. Considering the case of the Church with all leaders and not enough followership, what spiritual or organizational deficiencies, if any, result from such a predominance of leadership and invisible followership? What could a new pastor do in such a case to develop a more balanced culture that recognized followership and welcomed, valued, and developed the calling and spiritual gifts of following?

PART TWO

Acting On What You See

The Primal and Ultimate Organizational Power Is Effective Following

At the fall board meeting after I started as a vice president of Fresno Pacific College, now University, the president resigned, kicking off an international search for a replacement. By the following spring that process had produced no viable candidates. The search committee had asked me if I would consider the position, and I had resolutely declared that I was not the president I thought we needed.

They asked me to reconsider. I phoned my dad, retired from many years as a pastor and college and denominational administrator. He listened. Then with characteristic candor he said, "Well son, maybe you should try it, because otherwise you might end up working for an even worse president than you would be." We laughed together as we realized that his assessment could have two different meanings, but the point was made. I recanted.

The board soon reconvened, confirmed their interest in me, and developed an agreement about the corporate leap of faith that would lead to my appointment as a new kind of president for the organization. The institution was at a critical and vulnerable juncture, and we all sensed how important it was to get a competent manager and administrator who would also be an effective leader with enough support from all the key constituent groups.

With unspoken but impressive consensus, the board members acted in concert as though they knew what a leader was. They all seemed to be working with the same primary idea of a leader, but if you would have completed a survey of those board members, no such conceptual agreement could have been verified. Indeed, they disagreed sharply at times about what mattered most in the decision, and they were not unanimously enthusiastic about whether I was the right person. The employees were even more divided and ambivalent. But by some mysterious process, and without being able to agree on all the right words together, the board of trustees and the employees seemed to sense what they wanted and, perhaps more importantly, what they did not want.

The board could create a positional leader with an appropriate title, and they could give that positional leader the power to manage subordinates in the organization and direct the use of available resources. In that positional or formal context, everyone involved understood that the subordinates are positional followers who are under the authority of the person above them in the hierarchy. They are under obligation to do what their manager directs them to do, but they are a unique source of wisdom and effectiveness, and also a potential source of fatally uncommitted followership.

The board and every employee also understood, though mostly by an unexpressed sense of the latent logic of organizational life, that the board could not make any employee be a personally committed and enthusiastic follower and supporter of the new president. Each person inside the organization would make their own decision about how committed their followership would be.

The population of potential followers also included a lot of people outside the organization who were not on the university payroll and were not subordinate to the president and not obligated in any way to support. They were the customers, clients, business and political leaders, media, church members, donors, parents, and all the other constituents on whom the organization was absolutely dependent. The nagging and unanswerable question was who would and who would not voluntarily follow the leadership of a young, relatively unknown, and unproven president into uncomfortable new territory where they were not obligated to go. Each of those external persons would make their own individual decision about supporting the new "outsider" president. Each employee, volunteer, and potential financial partner or supporter would make their own decision about what kind and degree of commitment they would make to help the new president succeed.

From its position at the top of the corporate pyramid a board leads with power and sets policies and directives that determine the allocation of power within the organization. The person who holds the chief executive position is subordinate to the board and is, by logical necessity, the positional follower of the board. But the board members, individually and in concert with each other, accepted the importance of granting enormous authority and influence to the president as the organizational leader.

However, the board members did all the things effective followers must do for their leader to succeed. Thus, the board and the president simultaneously had to lead and follow each other. The trustees could not make anyone else choose to follow me, but they had one powerful way to help ensure their presidential appointment would be effective. From their position of leadership power, they chose to exercise the enormous power of leadership by example. As leaders they chose to follow the president. Their action demonstrated the foundational and insuperable power of voluntary personal followership. Such followership ultimately determines who leads and how successful that leader will be.

So, almost immediately began the conversation and experiences that produced a profound transformation of my understanding of organizational leadership. The board leaders told me that I was now the spiritual and organizational leader of the institution whose welfare had been entrusted to them for care and governance. Subsequently other board members came and personally expressed various versions of the same concept. They remained the official and legal leadership entity, but they were now delegating to me the responsibility and the authority to lead and manage their institution. They made it abundantly clear that this delegation meant I would be leading the entire institution, which meant that I would be leading them as the board, and they would be following my leadership. They assured me that they would retain and exercise their ultimate responsibility for the whole enterprise, including me as president; that they would constantly and rigorously evaluate my performance and the success of the whole organization; and that they would hold me accountable for its health, effectiveness, and success in service to the church for the Kingdom of God.

In varied ways they kept asking me the defining question that initiated and sustained the transformation—for me, for them, and for the organization, including every person served or in any way affected by its organizational effectiveness. It is the question that marks the expression of engaged and effective followership: What can we do to help you succeed as our leader?

I looked into the sincere faces of these highly capable people who could not in any way diminish their ultimate responsibility for the guidance and governance of an institution that they dearly loved and sacrificially supported. They carried their leadership responsibilities with a deep sense that they were truly serving God as they tried to make the organization express the will of God on earth.

In their professional roles some of them ran businesses that dwarfed Fresno Pacific at that point, and they were the highest level of authority and power in the organization. What I began to see with increasing clarity was that with this one question they each assumed the role of active follower in fulfillment of their leadership responsibility. I had never looked at organizational life that way before. What can we do to help you succeed?

The board members with the ultimate authority over the whole organization asked the primary question that an effective follower asks in a healthy organization. They had exercised their power to hire me, and they still held the concomitant power to fire me. Having hired me, they made me the leader by choosing to become my active and fully engaged followers. They committed themselves to my success, because if I succeeded as president that meant the organization would be a success and their sacred trust would be satisfied. But if I failed, so probably would their treasured but vulnerable institution. As the top leadership body, they would serve as my followers. They would guide me and hold me accountable, but also support me.

In a larger, wealthier, more robust organization the situation would have been just as true, but not nearly so obvious. And in an organization with a different culture of beliefs and values, one with a proud tradition of prosperity and a strong market position, it might not have been expressed so clearly and openly, nor with such authentic honesty and urgency. Indeed, it probably would not have been expressed at all. Their commitment to follow my leadership expressed the sort of genuine humility that comes from inner strength, not from weakness; from confidence and conviction, not from doubt or uncertainty; from concern for others, not from concern for self; and from a deep sense of stewardship rather than the prerogatives of ownership. And they were in no way abrogating their responsibility to direct my work, evaluate me, and hold me accountable, since those are key activities that effective followers perform for their leaders.

One by one, to varying degrees and in widely varied ways, most of them made the personal decision to do whatever they could to help their new president succeed. They voluntarily decided to follow the president. By actively doing the things that leaders need from their followers, the board members created a presidential leader with great authority and influence over themselves as the members of the board. In the years since then I have learned that we could have been more efficient and effective, if the board would have created two separate committees, one dedicated to evaluating and guiding my performance as their president, and one dedicated to supporting my emotional and spiritual welfare.

From centuries of reflection, experience, research, and writing one universal, comprehensible, and unarguable definition of a leader has emerged, a definition that is true for every kind of leader in every leadership situation, whether it is leading with formal power or leading without such power. The board ensured by their actions the most elemental principle of leadership.

A Leader Has Followers

The first words of Tom Atchison's book *Followership* are, "Leaders have followers. Being called the chief executive officer (CEO) and standing in front of a group does not in itself make anyone a leader."[7] Many effective leaders are not executives and many "executives" are not really leaders. Michael Maccoby says, "There is only one irrefutable definition of a leader, and that is *someone people follow*."[8] Peter Drucker and many others have come to the same conclusion. There is no simpler or more basic definition, and any definition that attempts to be more elaborate or elegant either cannot cover every possible situation that is correctly considered leadership, or it cannot exclude situations that purport to be leadership but are really something else. If nobody is following, then nobody is leading, and if nobody is leading then no leadership is happening. To the extent that people are following someone, that person is a leader. Leadership is defined by the existence of the followership that creates the leadership.

On this critical point reality turns conventional wisdom upside down. Leadership does not define followership. Followership defines leadership. Leaders do not make followers. Followers make leaders. This principle requires a corollary.

A Follower Has a Leader

When a person accepts the influence of another person, they make that person their leader for the particular situation in which they accept that influence. And unless and until they accept that person's influence in their life, they are not their follower and that other person is not their leader. One easy way to understand this reversal of the predominant logic is to look at the well-known story of Jesus choosing his apostles.

Jesus is widely regarded as one of the most successful leaders of all time. A billion Christian followers believe he is the greatest leader who has ever lived, and countless martyrs have followed him to their deaths at the hands of unbelievers. More than two thousand years after the time he lived on earth, people continue to follow him. But the simple reality is that, until Jesus returns to earth and establishes his ultimate reign with power and glory, all he can do is invite people to follow him. For several billion people Jesus is not a leader, and they may even view him as their antagonist. Jesus is not a leader for you until you accept his invitation and choose to follow him by accepting his influence in your life. Jesus cannot make someone become his follower. Rather, people make Jesus a leader by accepting his influence in their thinking and behavior. When they do so, the result is a relational process of leadership and followership.

So, the Board set aside some long and deeply cherished institutional traditions, practices, and relationships, and chose me as a cultural and denominational outsider to be their president. But they went further. They made me their leader. That led others to make the same decision. And that made all the difference.

However, it was also still true that when I accepted the offer of the board of Fresno Pacific to be the president, I became subordinate to the board. The term subordinate simply means "under orders." I agreed to be under the power, control, and direction of the board and to accept and respect their legitimate authority over me and the entire organization. More explicitly I agreed "to serve at the pleasure of the board." It is the most complete form of subordination that exists in most organizations. At any time and without the need for any private or public explanation, the board can decide that it is not in the best interest of the organization for the person who is serving as president to continue in that position, and that person can be removed from office.

The board made me the positional leader with the title of president and all the associated organizational authority and managerial power. By definition, all the employees became subordinate positional followers of the person with the title of president, the positional leader, and that in turn created a situation of positional leadership and followership. The employees had no choice in the matter. If they wanted to keep their jobs in the organization, they were obligated to function under the authority and power of the president.

Organizational subordination is unilateral, which simply means that no two parties can be subordinate to each other. I was subordinate to the board and therefore the board could not also be subordinate to me. Such formal or structural subordination cannot be a reciprocal or mutual relationship. In all types of incorporated organizations, the board is the ultimate legal entity and therefore it has commensurate power and authority over the organization. The board and the chief executive can and should respect each other, but a subordinate cannot be his own "boss," or the system is incapacitated by illogic. The main purpose of a managerial hierarchy is to distribute and fix power and responsibility to produce predictable outcomes from the whole system.

In the long run, no incorporated entity can be better than its board, unless the board is merely a symbolic or legally mandated place holder. However, sometimes it can take a painfully long run to prove that this principle about the defining role of governing boards is inviolably true whether the organization is a church, a for-profit, a nonprofit, a government agency, or some other type of organization. The board is responsible to ensure that the organization operates according to all applicable laws, regulations, and ethical standards, and the law vests the corresponding power in the board. No board of any incorporated entity can completely avoid its duty to lead with the power vested in a corporate board. The board is responsible for the character, quality, and public benefit of the organization in society. Leadership is a key factor for any organization, and the board has the ultimate power to work its will regarding corporate policies and executive leadership within the formal managerial structure of the organization.

The Fresno Pacific board took all the necessary legal, governance, and managerial actions. They could grant title and power within the organizational structure, and by empowering the chief executive in the top position in the managerial hierarchy they could create a positional leader. By doing so they made every employee a subordinate of the president, and thus they created de facto positional followers. All such managerial actions of a board illustrate and express the process of leading with power.

The board arranged the managerial situation so that every employee needed to comply with presidential directives, within the limits of the law and the corporate policies and plans approved by the board. In short, the board filled the position of chief executive at the top of the organizational hierarchy, and by doing so the board established the most powerful leadership and management position in the formal organizational bureaucracy.

The term leadership is very commonly and properly used to refer to such managerial situations that are based in the power that the organization confers on certain positions. In this context managers with legitimate organizational power are rightly considered and called leaders; they are leaders because they hold certain positions of power and decision-making authority in the formal managerial hierarchy. They are positional leaders. And that makes their subordinates positional followers.

Throughout that presidency the board, both collectively and as individuals, consistently supported me formally and personally with wise and powerful followership in a collaboration of leading and following that helped turn a small struggling college into a respected and successful regional university. Over a longer period of time a more complex version of interdependent following and leading eventually developed with the faculty and other staff. Together we all learned and relearned our roles as followers and leaders.

From the outside most people tended to assume that presidential leadership had produced a significant turnaround. From the inside, the quiet truth was that, despite my countless mistakes and some major blunders, a new paradigm was developing in which leading and following were two equally important and respected roles that everyone filled as needed in a collaborative process seeking a successful organization to strengthen the church and advance the Kingdom of God on earth.

An institution known for its egalitarian ethos had also become adept at "devouring its leaders," as one veteran professor described it. They learned how to see me as a potentially useful outsider that they previously would not have noticed or accepted. They learned how to see and support each

other in leading and following, and how to develop more effective following and leading at all levels. An organization that had valued servanthood
in its rhetoric had, in its practice, too often disregarded followership. Slowly
servant followers gained standing with servant leaders. They stepped out on
the long journey of learning to recognize, affirm, and intentionally develop
effective followership that openly speaks the truth in love and models a prophetic critique of any unhealthy organizational values, habits, or outcomes.
Their slogans became their strategies.

Effectiveness is achieving the desired condition.

The interplay of effective leading and effective following was practiced
and learned with slow but continuous improvement over time. Those who
were leading and those who were following learned to recognize the achievements of each role. The organizational culture was far from perfect, but the
necessary organizational structures, policies, and desired conditions, including a culture of confidence, were steadily emerging. In comparison with its
former character, the organization was transforming itself with a new direction and a new vision of its identity, its followership, its leadership, and its
future possibilities in the Church and in the work of God's Kingdom.

Leadership defines the job. Followership gets it done.

The president who preceded me led the institution through a decade
of progress at the price of difficult and often painful change and a personally exhausting labor of administrative and spiritual leadership. He and
the board and staff had successfully repositioned the institution during his
presidency, and then he had transitioned with impressive grace from mostly
leading the organization as the president to mostly following in administrative matters and leading students as a uniquely gifted professor. And no
person was a more effective professional and personal follower of my leadership than he was.

Summarizing the pace and direction of the transformation that had
started during his tenure and continued through mine, with his character-

istic wit and wisdom he asked me an intriguing question as I was finishing that presidency:

It seems to work in practice, but will it work in theory?

They are still working on the answer. But they have succeeded at increasing the dimensions of corporate diversity and growth while maintaining a firm community consensus about the key elements of their identity, core values, current reality, and the possibilities of their future. The cumulative changes became a transformation of the culture of the whole organization and created confidence for a new future vision. That vision included the arduous process of learning to see following and leading as equally important interdependent roles that each person needed to master and respect.

Strong, effectively engaged followership creates and sustains effective leadership. It is constantly being learned and it is always happening imperfectly, but when you are consciously working out your prayer for God's Kingdom to come (now) and God's will to be done (now) on earth as it (already) is in heaven, then one element of following and leading on earth here and now is unavoidable:

Imperfection is the only option.

Meditation

> One day as Jesus was walking along the shore of the Sea of Galilee, he saw two brothers—Simon, also called Peter, and Andrew—throwing a net into the water, for they fished for a living. Jesus called out to them, "Come, follow me, and I will show you how to fish for people!" And they left their nets at once and followed him.
>
> A little farther up the shore he saw two other brothers, James and John, sitting in a boat with their father, Zebedee, repairing their nets. And he called them to come, too. They immediately followed him, leaving the boat and their father behind. (Matthew 4:18-22)

By accepting the invitation that Jesus offered to them, these four men made Jesus an earthly leader. At that critical moment in the cosmos, he was the unique Son of God and Son of Man, King of the Jews, the one true Sovereign over all creation, Commander of gigantic Angel Armies, King of the entire Kingdom of God. But in the earthly realm, Jesus was not a leader of people until that day when those four men agreed to follow him. When you decide to follow Jesus, you make Jesus your leader.

When you decide to follow someone by trusting their influence in your life, you make that person your leader. The definition of a follower is a person who has chosen their leader, just as the definition of a leader is a person who has followers. The great power of followership is creating and supporting leadership. And the great work of following is supporting and advancing the success of the leader in achieving their shared mission, vision, and values.

Talking with God

Heavenly Father, purify my passion and clarify my commitment to do everything I can to advance the purposes of my one true and perfect leader, Jesus Christ, and the greatness of his Kingdom. For that to happen I need you to give me special wisdom in choosing the people I should follow. Enhance my efforts to help make those leaders more effective so that we will together make our human organizations serve the greatness of your kingdom on earth as it is in heaven. Amen.

Questions and Issues

A. In what ways is it true and not true that effective fully engaged followers have the ultimate power in an organization?

B. In electoral democracies the persons in top legislative and executive leadership positions are chosen by a majority of the voters. But that means that a large minority does not want to follow the person who won the election. What does it mean for the winners and the losers in this case to seek first the Kingdom of God?

C. In the implementation of following and leading, in government or other settings, what is the meaning and practical relevance of being "the loyal opposition?" What conditions would make it impossible or indefensible to remain "loyal"?

D. How do you separate following or leading as an identity—who you are—from following and leading as roles—what you do? Why does this distinction matter?

E. What human needs elicit the perfection drive? What techniques or practices can help prevent the noble desire for perfection from producing inefficiency that results in ineffectiveness?

F. What factors matter the most to you in your process of choosing and supporting a leader?

Full and Effective Delegation Makes You a Follower

As soon as the board of Fresno Pacific made the public announcement of my appointment to the presidency (the first of two tenures separated by 17 years), my immediate urgency was to have the best possible executive team in place and functioning for the next academic year that would begin in four months. Some positions were empty, including the one I was vacating to become president. Some areas needed restructuring with changed assignments, and some key people needed to be convinced or confirmed to stay. The board gave me authority to make employment commitments during the interim while I was still vice president and also president-elect. I had a modest budget and a short timeline.

I came to realize that in every instance the core of a wise decision depended on coming to an unambiguous shared understanding of the same four interdependent elements that had grounded the board's negotiation and agreement with me. Each person who agreed to join the leadership team became part of the process of discerning who the other team members should be and how we would all work together. It was abundantly obvious that each one of us depended on all the others. All subsequent leadership appointments sought clarity on the same four basic elements of those delegation assignments. And those same elements also framed the subsequent evaluations of their individual effectiveness and the success of the team as a whole.

1. Current reality: An accurate vision of the current organizational reality, including the reality of their proposed area of responsibility in particular.

2. Desired future: The desired conditions they would be responsible to achieve and the date when it should be done.

3. Authority and responsibility: The leadership authority and fol-lowership responsibility that I would delegate to them to help achieve those desired conditions.

4. Resources: The organizational personnel and resources that would and would not be under their managerial control.

In some cases it was difficult to convince the person that I was actually delegating to them the primary leadership responsibility in their area of the organization. Some of them returned repeatedly to an emphasis on their desire to follow my leadership as president and to affirm in various ways their intention to understand what I wanted and help make it happen. That assurance of what is commonly called loyalty is important, and I needed to be able to trust them to be loyal. Insubordination can destroy a leader or an organization, and sometimes that is its intended result. But in certain situa-tions, an action that is technically insubordination can save an organization from a disastrous blunder. I was determined to ensure that they understood that I was *not* asking them to be silent obedient followers of the president.

Instead, I needed them to understand that I was authorizing and ex-pecting them to lead the organization in their area of responsibility, and that I was committing myself to follow their lead. I would try to understand their part of the organization as well as I could and do whatever I could in my role as president to help them succeed in coordination with all the other managers. That is the work of following.

The work of following is helping someone else succeed.

And that meant that I was depending on them to hold me accountable and to always tell me the truth about anything they thought I ought to know for the good of the cause, regardless of how it might affect me personally or professionally.

We were trying to achieve the same inversion of leading and follow-ing that I was experiencing with the board. I was delegating my leadership responsibility and authority to them on the assumption that it was their responsibility to understand their area better than I did. The board and the organization needed me to succeed as president. And as their president I would need to skillfully serve each of them as their fully engaged and supportive follower. In most cases it took many months of practice until each one understood that I was truly serious about it. I persisted in that process with those who reported to me, partly because I was trying to master the same model with the board.

Highly effective leaders do a lot of follower work.

We all were intensely aware that we were facing enormous challenges to our survival, stability, and progress, and we needed more and better leadership than I could provide by myself, and more than each of us could provide with maximum effort. To have any chance of succeeding we needed synergy to amplify every bit of highly effective leadership we could develop. That pressing reality required me to be their follower and thus create more leadership, while they were also following me in the necessary leadership work of my presidential role.

It was no surprise that we often asked each other some form of the same question: What can I do to help you succeed? It is the effective follower's question.

Follower Case: I Want People to Make Me Successful

Elena was talking with her faculty advisor in the school of education as they planned the schedule of courses she would need to complete to obtain her teaching credential. As they finished, the prof summarized the distinctive attractions of a career in the teaching profession. The prof described teaching as a uniquely respected leadership profession in society, partly because, in contrast to most other professions, teachers are dedicated to the advancement and success of other people rather than to their own fame and fortune. Ideally, teachers want their students to achieve even more than their teachers did.

A few days later Elena withdrew from the school of education and transferred into a business program. Her parents and other family members were surprised. When they inquired about the sudden and significant change of plans, she said very simply, "I don't want to help other people succeed and get ahead of me. I want people to follow me and make me successful."

She was probably prudent to leave the field of education, but her subsequent career in business was limited to her knowledge and skills as she directed the activities of her subordinates. She could not see it as mutual following and leading with everyone developing together.

Meditation

> Then the eleven disciples left for Galilee, going to the mountain where Jesus had told them to go. When they saw him, they worshiped him—but some of them doubted!
>
> Jesus came and told his disciples, "I have been given all authority in heaven and on earth. Therefore, go and make disciples of all the nations, baptizing them in the name of the Father and the Son and the Holy Spirit. Teach these new disciples to obey all the commands I have given you. And be sure of this: I am with you always, even to the end of the age." (Matthew 28:16-20)

As he left the earth, Jesus Christ put his followers in charge of advancing his Kingdom in his absence. He said he would be with them, work with them, support them, and encourage them. He could even work miracles for them at times, but he would not lead them in any normal visible way. He gave them a clear and simple description of what they should accomplish and the values that should guide their choices. But they would have to organize and figure out how to do it.

Taken together, the three synoptic Gospels provide considerable detail about what is commonly called the Great Commission, the comprehensive final guidance that Jesus gave to his disciples just before he left them and was taken up into heaven. As so easily and naturally happens, in focusing on what Jesus said, it is easy to miss the fact of what he did not say. In a variety of ways Jesus had told the eleven disciples what they were supposed to accomplish in the world. He promised to be with them in the work of sharing the Good News of new life in Christ and his Kingdom. But he did not say he would lead them in the particulars of that process. He repeatedly told them to be humble servants in seeking to advance the values and ideals of his Kingdom. He specifically did not tell them to become leaders or to try to use political or personal power to make people behave properly for the Kingdom.

Instead, Jesus declared that all the kingdom authority had been given to him, and he delegated that leadership authority to the inner circle of his followers with the assurance that he would be with them and the others that they would recruit, or as the Gospel of Mark expresses it, he would "work with them." He delegated the leadership of his kingdom on earth to them during his absence, and he promised that he would do the work of a follower. He would be present with them, support them, and work with them.

The Creator and King of everything that exists in space and time delegated the mission of advancing his Kingdom on earth to his eleven disciples, and he assumed the role of their fully engaged and supportive follower. He promised to be faithfully present and supportive. He directed them to wait for the coming of his Holy Spirit before they began their efforts. Their role was to organize and lead the effort and he assumed the role of their invisible follower. It is the role he will continue to fill until he returns to fully assert his power and authority as the King of earth and heaven.

Talking with God

Jesus, You are the one true King and by your saving grace I am your servant-follower, working to advance your Kingdom. As you left the earth, you delegated leadership of the greatest mission of all to your faulty human followers, including me. You are my Savior and my King, but you are also my servant-follower. Help me understand how this interaction of leading and following needs to work for me in each of my organizations and relationships. Strengthen the spirit of humility in me so I will always be learning for the benefit of others, not proudly hoping for a place of honor in your Kingdom or in this world's system.

Because you are eternally my Savior and my one true and perfect leader, I want to seek the greatness of your Kingdom as effectively as I can. You are not physically present here now, so I depend on the whispered wisdom and encouragement of your Holy Spirit to know the particulars of every decision in my role as a follower or a leader. Especially when I have leader-work to do, teach me how to be a fully engaged and highly effective follower, as you are with me. Amen.

Questions and Issues

A. What other elements may need to be explicit in the delegation of a leadership assignment in addition to the basic four listed here?

B. Is it possible to delegate a followership assignment or responsibility? If not, why? If so, what would be an example?

C. What is the ideal response of a leader when a subordinate leader makes a major mistake that produces failure to achieve a key delegated objective?

D. Is there a place for partial delegation where the leader can over-rule?

E. How do you evaluate the student's decision and rationale in the follower case? Was it wise self-insight? Self-centered? Immature? Courageous? Admirably honest?

Effective Leading Moves an Organization to a New Condition

You do not need effective leadership to stay where you are and keep doing what you have been doing. You do not need effective leadership to end up with whatever the current reality happens to become. But you do need effective leadership for intentional change to experience a condition you want to exist that is not likely to happen on its own and that may not even be clearly visible.

A desired future condition is a definable, describable, and measurable reality that the members of an organization want to experience together. It is not a vague or ephemeral hope, a direction or path, or even a lofty goal that inspires and energizes everyone to "do your best and the closer to it we end up, the better." It is a particular place that the organization wants to reach and celebrate together on its path to its chosen future. The condition could be something that the whole organization is aware of, works collaboratively to achieve, and rejoices to experience together, like being ranked in the top five nationally, or ending the fiscal year in the black three times in a row for the first time ever. Or the desired condition could be a critical new system that is developed in secret and flawlessly installed at midnight by a handful of people with no public announcement. A desired condition can be internal or external; holistic or very particular. An internal desired condition is something the organization wants to become. An external desired condition is something the organization wants to be true for the people it serves. Experiencing the full glory of the Kingdom of God is a desired condition, and so is the joy of five years clean and sober by the alcoholic parents of two healthy children. Both these beautiful conditions display the results of godly effective following and leading.

Sometimes a significant desired condition happens for an organization mostly by fortuitous accident, independently from or even in spite of the person who has the leadership position or title. Often that positional leader or someone else will claim or be given leadership credit for achieving the desired condition. This occurs in organizations of all sizes, from nation-states to families. Wise followers know the difference between leading intentional change to achieve a chosen goal and taking credit for favorable conditions and outcomes that happened by the goodness of God's grace.

You need a lot more than effective leading to intentionally make a new reality happen, no matter how great or small the change may be. But leadership is normally an essential element, and God delights when wise and effective followers choose and support wise and effective leaders for his Kingdom. At its heart, leading is about intentional internal change to become something different or external change to achieve something in the world outside the organization. Ideally the new condition is something better than what was left behind, but, unfortunately, improvement according to the values of the Kingdom of God is not essential to the definition of leadership for change. Too often an autocratic or narcissistic leader moves the organization to an unhealthy condition that unjustly favors some people at the expense of others, but never without unhealthy followers.

Different results require seeing, thinking, and acting differently.

Proposing and planning organizational change is a leadership function. That fact does not mean that only people with leadership positions or titles can propose change. Instead, it means that whoever proposes a change is performing a leadership function, regardless of their job description or title. A decisive element of your current organizational reality is the demonstrated organizational culture and capacity for wise change, including the ability to let go of the present and the wisdom to know when to let go and when not to. Change depends on learning, and learning starts with humility, the humble and hopeful admission of your ignorance and your desire to see and understand things differently and work for change to make things better.

Changing the organization is mostly a followership function. The members of your organization may not be satisfied with the current reality or the expected future reality results of your organizational efforts, or both. But in practice it is typical to see little, if any, eagerness to consider or embrace change unless there is a sense of urgency. Resistance to change is an assumption in every theory of organizational or individual development. Resistance to change is an important followership function, so followers must decide if and when to redirect their energy from questioning and resisting a proposed change to supporting and working to achieve it.

Followers find it easier to change leaders than to change themselves. "Insanity is doing the same thing over and over and expecting different results" (according to Benjamin Franklin, and many others). It is a particular kind of organizational madness that often afflicts people acting as followers: to keep repeating the same behaviors that are based on the same assumptions and beliefs, while hoping against the odds that this time it will work. The working assumption is: If there is a major problem you just need to get better leadership so everything will improve. There are two common ways to get better leadership: change the current leader (with some form of leadership training or development) or get a new and different type of leader (with some form of a leadership search process). Either way, the assumption is that the solution is to keep changing leaders till you get the leadership you need.

Sometimes the great-leader model seems to work for a while, and hope lures people onward. You need and want your organization to succeed, so you need your leaders to succeed. Leaders need time to produce the desired improvement, so, except in polarized political environments, new or revised leaders are customarily given a grace period to show what they can accomplish. For the new CEO of the company, the new principal at the school, the new pastor at church, the new boss at work, or the new president of the nation, people hope they will succeed so everyone benefits. The obvious change is the new leader. The unobvious change is on the part of the followers.

Bernard Bass summarizes this principle in his masterwork on leadership. "Indeed, leadership is often regarded as the single most critical factor in the success or failure of institutions."[9] But the reality is that an overly narrow, magnified, or otherwise distorted focus on leaders and leadership that ignores followers and followership sooner or later produces inadequate results that force the search for a new leadership to simply repeat the process. The dominant leader-centric paradigm is fundamentally flawed, and the time between changing leaders tends to shorten while the economic and human cost of each failure increases.

You can keep repeating the same patterns based on the same assumptions, but it is madness or folly to expect that you will somehow magically get different results. The alternative requires different values operating in a different paradigm on different assumptions. Getting different organizational conditions does not necessarily require getting different leaders. But it does require different thinking. "We can't solve problems by using the same kind of thinking we used to create them" (Albert Einstein).

A simplistic leader-centric perspective gets you into this situation, and clinging to that same kind of thinking will keep you there. Thinking differently about how to get the desired conditions you need from your organization is essential for being truly healthy for the members of the organizations and for all the people that the organization exists to serve. Typically, passive, silent, or sullen followership is often the unidentified underlying cause, which is often masked with masterful verbosity by and about leadership. "When you don't know what you are talking about, it's hard to know when you're finished" (Tommy Smothers).

Without a working consensus on adequate definitions of leading and following, or a paradigm that integrates these two core elements of organizational life, you cannot know what you are talking about. That ignorance leads you to bravely press on with an endless flow of books, articles, trainings, consultations, and meetings about leading as though it were the primary source of organizational excellence, rather than the product of following. Given a leader-centric culture without a unifying core concept of leadership, there is an endless flood of spoken and written words about it. The thought-field that is centered on leadership is huge. An Amazon search gave over sixty thousand results for a search on leadership books (including my own book, *Leadership Prayers*), and that figure does not include all the books that contain some aspect of leadership in marketing, human resources, and every other possible aspect of organizational life.

By contrast, an Amazon search for "followership books" indicated 461 results. And that set included under "followership" titles such as *Followership: Leading from Behind* and *Leading So People Will Follow*. The thought-field on followership is comparatively recent and small, but a spacious, well-grounded, and actionable framework has been developed for a robust understanding of the many kinds of followership on which all leadership ultimately depends. The combination of the two intertwined fields of following and leading provides the different kind of thinking that is needed to see organizational problems and weaknesses in new, more complete ways and improve the likelihood of progress. Effective following and leading together can enable you to see what really exists and what must be done for your organization to be healthy for everyone involved, and also be financially and competitively successful.

Beware of the seduction of servant leadership.

Unfortunately, many people who refer to servant leadership have not read the book with that title in which Robert Greenleaf originally coined the term and explained the concept, or any of the other subsequent publications.[10] So, it is no surprise that such an attractive phrase has been given various meanings and applications to advance diverse realities, visions, and purposes. Some have made a positive difference in collaborative power sharing and commitment to the well-being of the followers. And some have not been as noble as the original call to lead as a humble servant for the good of others. It can instead be a disguised version of traditional command-and-control leadership under which followers exist to serve the desires of the leader.

A true servant leader is humble enough to learn from their followers. Being humble in spirit does not mean you are weak. In fact, to say that someone is a weak leader is to say they are not really leading. The same is true of followers. A weak follower is not an effective follower. Authentically humble leaders and followers are confident enough to admit mistakes, acknowledge ignorance, and take responsibility for learning and changing. A humble person who is also strong and confident can invest themselves in the success and welfare of someone else, and that is the work of followership. Authentically practicing the role of leading as a humble servant of the followers rather than for personal gain or advancement is a kingdom-seeking posture.

Greenleaf did not formulate or explain his theory as an expression of Christian theology or Biblical authority, but the Church and its partner organizations and movements have been attracted to the principles he propounded, including humility, collaborative interdependence, and mutual benefit.

However, the Church and other organizations of Christendom have not consistently recognized the limits of leading like Jesus when imperfect human followers and leaders try to implement Greenleaf's principles. Servant leaders rightly involve their followers in setting standards of performance and evaluating effectiveness. But Jesus alone determines the standards and judges the performance of his followers in his Kingdom. Because Jesus is the omniscient and perfect leader, the Kingdom of Jesus Christ is appropriately leader-centric in a divinely spiritual way that is foolish and counter-productive in all other lesser organizations. Jesus' followers seek to know and do what Jesus wants. A human leaders' power comes from their followers, but the Kingdom of God is the reverse. Christ gives power to his followers, enabling them to be effective stewards of kingdom resources as they seek first the Kingdom of God.

Thus, with many important and successful exceptions, the Church and its various parachurch agencies, orders, and organizations too often demonstrate the same leader-centric values and structures as the secular society that they seek to influence and serve. Too often Christian servant leaders "serve" their followers by discerning what God wants and telling the followers what to do and how to do it. Churches and their organizations do lots of leadership development training and honoring, but rarely any real followership development or recognition, other than an emphasis on following Jesus in your personal life, and then obeying and supporting your human leader.

In sharp contrast to this pattern, R. Scott Rodin provides a robust, theologically sound, and beautifully practical understanding of what is possible "when a godly steward is called to lead."[11] The Kingdom of God is a perfectly ordered organization of followers supporting their leaders in collaborative stewardship of all creation under the King's sovereign authority and for his glory. Seeking Godly steward leadership is an excellent way to disclose and correct the inauthentic and unhealthy versions of leadership.

Despite the repeated statements of Jesus about serving and following each other and not adopting the power patterns of the surrounding secular culture, the Church globally and locally too often focuses on leadership development and ignores followership development. It commonly operates in deference to who has the most power or celebrity—or the most fragile ego—rather than prioritizing what is wise and good for the whole community and the Kingdom. When Christ-centered people of faith do get it right, whether in a churchly or a secular setting, they are a mighty force for good in the world. Authentic humility is the basic requirement for understanding the wisdom of the Holy Spirit in the process of leading change as stewards of the King's resources.

The concept of servant-leadership resonates with the stated values of most people of faith, and often with others as well. The term suggests altruism and emphasizes generous giving rather than selfish taking. But servant-leadership often is distorted into a seductive rhetorical device that is employed to avoid the notion of needing to follow or support another person. The ultimate emphasis tends to remain on being the leader rather than being a servant. A true servant-leader is supposed to lead with a humble, selfless heart, one who is committed to the welfare of all the people who are in the organization or served by it. A noble leader advances the organization toward its desired future by serving everyone, including by serving them in the role of follower as well as leader. A true servant-leader is equally a servant-follower.

The proverb says that pride precedes a failure, but when pride looks and feels normal and noble in a leader, and maybe even necessary to ensure success, then the concomitant leadership faults and failures also seem normal and noble, and thus excusable. This tragic blunder is especially tempting and common when the leader is a high-profile "Christian celebrity" among key constituencies and markets, with a public persona that is essential to the reputation and financial success of the organization. In these cases, the organization exists to serve the leader, rather than the leader being a true servant-follower with a unique servant-leadership role to fill. The board, staff, and other followers may sincerely come to believe that their servant-leader is above every doubt or suspicion, must be protected at all costs from every accusation, and must be trusted absolutely without verification regardless of any questionable quirk of behavior or expenditure. In a healthy and successful organization, the members can safely trust each other's integrity.

Trust is the child of integrity and competence.

Integrity is the product of verified capacity to perform as expected.

Integrity is being what you claim to be and what you allow others to claim or to think about you. And integrity is keeping every commitment, always doing what you say you will do, and alerting others any time your performance might be below or significantly above expectations. Authentic integrity welcomes and cooperates fully with authentic verification.

A true servant-leader is never bigger or more important than the mission, vision, and values that the organization exists to advance. These principles must be inviolable in a Kingdom-modeled organization, and they must be applied by wise servant-followers, including when those followers must also be wise servant-leaders.

Thus, for all kinds of organizations, from global corporations and governments to local churches, nonprofits, and marriages, the humble heart of a creative learner is a basic requirement. But humility alone does not produce the desired organizational health and success. The process of leading with a follower's humble heart also requires enormous inner confidence, strength, courage. We may not see the leadership we should choose to follow because it is hidden behind the plain cloak of humility.

The noble concept of servant-leadership is too often twisted to make room for leaders who are inherently proud but are actually weak or ineffective commanders, rather than humble but strong servants who take on the role of leading for the good of the group. Jesus was not modest; he made outlandish claims about himself. But he was humble, and he was definitely not weak or self-serving. He immodestly claimed to be God's son, the divinely anointed Messiah, the way to God, the truth of God, and the very life of God. He was a leader who came to serve, not to be served. He lived and died serving others and helping them succeed as leaders and followers after he departed. With intentional insight you can recognize and follow the authentic version of the servant who leads out of humility, and who brings strength, courage, meaning, and hope to the followers. But a competent leader with the heart of a true servant and steward is not sufficient to ensure a healthy and successful organization. At least four other elements are necessary for moving out from the fortress of leadership supremacy into the world of collaborative, interdependent, effective following and leading.

1. Wise Values

Identify the controlling values and behaviors that got you where you are, and systematically make wiser choices that will allow you to move past the present impasse to achieve organizations that people trust because they serve well. Values are principles, beliefs, or standards that matter enough to you that they guide your behavior. What matters to you about an organization affects what you do in relation to that organization. No matter how indefensibly wrong a situation may appear, every organizational condition can exist only if enough people value something about that condition strongly enough. The leader-centric model is the default pattern that most people can see, understand, and value. But wiser values can prevail when followers require it.

2. Healthy Intolerance

Refuse to accept that ineffective organizations and/or inadequate leadership are the best you can hope for. Become proactively intolerant of the mediocrity that results when unhealthy organizations allow undeveloped followers to select inadequate leaders who do not merit our trust and support. Your role in the organization influences the nature and expression of your mistrust, but to the extent that you cannot truly trust, you must restrain your followership.

As voters, consumers, stockholders and all other kinds of owners, donors, volunteers, legislators, managers, administrators, students, taxpayers, and in all the other roles that you might assume, call each other to more than the minimalist contract of mediocrity. Commit to the covenant ideal of the highest reasonable standard of individual and corporate effectiveness. In every kind of organization, Christian or secular, claim your determining role as follower, and never settle for inadequate leadership and invisible followership. In organizations built on principles of religious faith and values, remember that sanctimonious shoddy is still shoddy.

3. Success That Benefits Everyone

Require your organizations to be healthy, not just financially healthy but holistically healthy, with environments in which healthy people can contribute their gifts and talents to achieve significant and satisfying outcomes.

Success is defined as reaching your goal, achieving your desired condition. Moving forward, the real definition of organizational success must include being a healthy organization in which the members become better people: more skillful, more fulfilled, more joyful, more like their Creator. It turns out that successful organizations are morally, emotionally, relationally, and spiritually healthy, and that is what makes them successful competitors.

4. Honesty about Evil

Employ an adequate and honest definition of what the leadership and followership process really is in the organization and how people actually function in the leader and follower roles. To do this, avoid your natural temptation to think that the only real following and leading that exists is good following and leading. Incompetence, self-service, and corruption are constant dangers that are often well disguised. Bad leadership is not just imperfect leadership; it is flawed and damaging leadership that prevents human flourishing. You must accurately describe your reality, and then you can separately prescribe the kind of organization you need. When you pretend that the only true leadership is morally good and competent leadership, you make it easier for bad leaders and their complicit followers to gain power that looks legitimate.

Leading and following are extremely important for every person, but you must be careful to maintain definitions of leadership and followership that describe the full range of what they actually are, so that a healthy organization will not inadvertently reward or even tolerate the toxic leading or following that distorts the vision and subverts the values of the Kingdom of God and unjustly supports toxic organizational dysfunction.

Meditation

> Don't copy the behavior and customs of this world, but let God transform you into a new person by changing the way you think. Then you will learn to know God's will for you, which is good and pleasing and perfect. (Romans 12:2)

Every organization on earth operates in the unhealthy context of the values, behaviors, and customs of a secular world system. This reality is true for every type and size of organization, from a nuclear family, which is the smallest and most common type of organizational unit, to nations, multinational corporations, multinational alliances like NATO and the United Nations, and everything in between, including informal organizations and religious organizations, including your local congregation.

The ultimate power behind this pervasive world system is Satan, the dedicated enemy of Christ, and this world system is the manifestation of the kingdom of Satan, whose purposes and values seek to constrain, contradict, distort, and nullify every aspect of the Kingdom of God. Copying the behaviors, customs, and truths of this world system is, therefore, a constant temptation. Everything from the legal regulations to the power of public opinion constantly presses every thought and action toward the benefits of conformity with the dominant culture.

Confident faith is required for you to let God change the way you think and feel, especially when the system typically tries to define financial success in opposition to what is truly and eternally healthy for every person in your organization or affected by it. God's good and pleasing and perfect will for you and your organization can be hard to see and even harder to accomplish.

Talking with God

May the words of my mouth and the meditation of my heart be pleasing to you, O Lord, my rock and my redeemer (Psalm 19:14). It is so easy and seems so smart to just adapt to the ecology of the world system. In my following and my leading I need to think and speak and value people differently so I can help us move to the new condition we must achieve. How do we discern what is the humble wisdom of your Kingdom and what is the proud folly of this world? Change the way I see things. Change the way I think, so I can help all of us together be more perfectly conformed to your Kingdom instead of the kingdoms of this world. Give me the voice and the heart to make this possible. Amen.

Questions and Issues

A. How can you discern the difference between authentic humility and false modesty in an actual or potential leader? When might this discernment be critical?

B. Why is change resistance so universal in organizational development? What are the benefits of resisting that make it so attractive and powerful to the followers?

C. As a follower, when change is proposed, how do you determine when you should resist the proposed change and when you should accept and support the proposed change?

D. Leaders seeking support for a proposed change may amplify fear, insecurity, or other negative emotions; use selective or distorted information to ignore risks or negative effects; and demean, demonize, or dehumanize other organizations or people groups. As a follower, what is your responsibility, if any, to try to independently verify or critique your leader's assumptions and assertions? How do you do so without seeming to be disloyal and risking your professional future if your doubts are disproved?

E. What are the best ways to learn and improve followership effectiveness?

No One Leads Alone

F ollowers determine who is a leader and who is not by deciding whom they will follow and whom they will not follow. The shared values and characteristics of any group of followers will be apparent in the leader they choose and how effectively they support that leader. Understandably, followers consider a good leader to be someone who matches their values, acknowledges or satisfies their felt needs, or moves toward a shared vision or purpose. Followers choose and support a leader who gives the followers what they want, and what the followers want grows out of who the followers are, what they believe is true or wish were true, and what really matters to them. No one leads alone.

A follower is anyone who accepts the influence of another person in their life, and that influencer is a leader of that follower. The influence usually includes how the follower sees reality, how they think, what they believe is true and not true, what is good and bad, and ultimately what all the followers do as the members of the organization. Over time the process of accepting the leader's influence makes the organization increasingly become an expression of who the leader is. But simultaneously, followers also influence and shape their leader. They must move together, and that requires followers and leaders to share similar notions of what their shared purpose is, what matters and what doesn't, and, in simplest terms, what is good and bad for people, and what marks a good or bad follower or leader.

The words good and bad are often used as summative descriptors of leaders and followers, but both words have multiple meanings and thus always need to be defined for each particular case. Some of the most obvious and common meanings relate to some version of being effective. A good leader gets the job done, makes things happen, or achieves key goals. A person is considered a good leader if the organization is marked by financial success or high morale or a positive image in the marketplace. But good (or bad) also often mean morally or ethically good. Good or bad for people.

The list of possible leadership characteristics or abilities is long. But confident and convincing communication—spoken and/or written—is consistently considered one of the most important indicators. Communication skill is so important in leading that often a person who is mainly—or only— an effective communicator is mistakenly presumed to be competent for leadership. In addition, communication skill is related to several other popular markers of an effective leader, including being visionary, relational, inspirational, well liked, and even trustworthy.

Typically, some dimension of appropriate morals and/or ethics is assumed in the concept of a good leader, but it is often left unstated, sometimes even in formal job descriptions and searches for leadership positions. Ideally, morally good and competent leaders are chosen and supported by morally good and competent followers who share a commitment to achieving a healthy desired condition that is truly good for everyone.

But leading and following are morally and ethically neutral concepts that require clarifying modifiers and context. Sometimes a leader moves an organization—which could be a whole nation—in a wrong direction by infusing the wrong values and rewarding behavior that produces a wrong future. Sometimes the condition is immorality, corruption, disaster, human suffering, war, or even organizational collapse or demise. Such ignoble leadership is not what most people call truly good leadership, but it is effective leadership nevertheless, and history provides countless examples of such morally bad leadership that was enabled by correspondingly bad followership. The sad irony is that the followers must believe that what is happening is good—at least for themselves—while it is happening, otherwise they would not willingly or effectively enable the leader to make it happen. *The Dictator's Handbook*[12] uses well documented real-world cases to describe the ways that autocratic leaders create and corruptly reward the followers they need to gain *and* maintain the power they need to assert their will over a nation or other type of organization for the undeserved and unjust benefit of their followers and themselves.

Ugly beauty may be an oxymoron that does not really exist, but there definitely is such a thing as bad leadership. Barbara Kellerman explores and explains this ugly reality in a way that dispels the contention of some people that bad leadership is not really leadership at all. Bad leadership is still leadership, and her compelling scholarship requires any comprehensive framework to allow for this very real dark side of the leadership phenomenon that bad followership makes possible.[13]

Leadership can be positive or negative, morally good or bad. Some leaders are dysfunctional, toxic, immoral, corrupt, mentally ill, abusive, inept, or self-serving. The list is as long and sad as the list of human failings. There is a bad version of just about every type of leadership. To suggest that the bad versions of leadership are not really leadership at all mistakenly simplifies the model by ignoring the obvious. Bad leadership does exist, and it is just as real and just as important as good leadership. And badly flawed leadership depends on badly flawed followership.

Things are the way they are because someone wants them that way.

Tomas Chamorro-Premuzic asks and answers a key question about why so many organizations and their leaders perform so badly, and this question is also the title of his book: *Why do so many incompetent men become leaders?*[14] He develops compelling evidence and logic that incompetent organizational leadership is widespread and that most of these incompetent leaders are men. Given that followers do in fact choose their leaders, and that their choices express who the followers are and what they really (often subconsciously) want, he addresses an unavoidable related question: Why is it so hard for competent people—especially competent women—to rise in corporate leadership hierarchies?

Combining his decades of multicultural experience with solid research findings, Chamorro-Premuzic contends that men make up a majority of leaders, but they underperform when compared with female leaders. In fact, followers in most organizations equate leadership potential with demonstrably destructive personality traits, like overconfidence and narcissism. Thus, the traits that help someone get selected for a leadership role prevent great leadership once the person has the job. When competent women—and men who don't fit the stereotype—are unfairly overlooked, everyone suffers the consequences, the members of the organization and the people the organization exists to serve. The result is a system of deeply flawed followership that prefers similarly flawed leadership.

Feckless followers admire arrogance rather than humility, mistake confidence for competence, and trust loud aggression over rational expertise and respectful wisdom in those to whom they grant leadership authority. Indeed, narcissistic followers want a narcissistic leader. Chamorro-Premuzic describes in carefully constructed detail what it really takes to lead well and how better systems and processes can help develop healthy and competent followers who put the right people in charge. His insights support the conceptual basis of effective following and leading. Wherever there is leadership to achieve any desired condition, there is corresponding followership that approves, sustains, and enables that leadership and that shares in the results.

Emotionally healthy and competent leaders and psychopathically narcissistic autocrats—of nations, corporations, churches, or personality cults—all depend on a base of followers who believe that the leader and the vision of desired conditions they share with that leader are good for them as followers. But there is one big problem. Maccoby states it succinctly. "The leaders we want are not always the leaders we need. . . . People continue to elect inept and corrupt leaders."[15] He points to the Israelites who wanted a king like the nations around them and suffered for it from then on. Just as it takes wise and competent followers to make a wise and competent leader successful, it takes corrupt followers to give power to a corrupt leader, immoral followers to sustain an immoral leader, and small-minded, self-centered, greedy, or fear-based followers to justify and maintain a leader in their own likeness who will give them the particulars they require at the expense of a truly healthy organization that successfully serves the greater good of everyone involved. Likewise, leaders who seek outcomes for the Kingdom of God must have followers who seek the same outcomes, though they may not seek them from the same ground of faith.

Chamorro-Premuzic and Maccoby use different data and conceptual frameworks to reach a similar explanation for the preference followers display for certain kinds of dominant male leaders. Leading and following are learned in childhood, primarily at home, so both males and females are subconsciously drawn to satisfy the need for transference to a confident, commanding, powerful father-figure for the role of leader. That tendency is strengthened by transference to the leader of the latent narcissistic desire to be in control, be most important, demean others, feel superior to others, and get one's own way.

Unfortunately, the fear-based transactional model of following and leading exploited in dictatorships has become normalized in partisan political democracies. The same pattern is prevalent in other kinds of organizations that operate under that government or depend on government funding, tax benefits, or legal protection, including in education and health care, and sadly also within the Church and Christian organizations. You can see the difference when you look carefully at what really matters in the process of making organizational decisions. Is the priority on power with selected transactional beneficiaries, or is it on compelling truth and justice to benefit everyone? Is it the special interests of leaders and particular followers, or is it a worthy shared mission, inclusive vision, and exemplary values? Does the titled leader serve the organization with humble, authentic, transparent accountability, or does the organization exist to serve the leader?

Truly good leaders are supported by good followers who share a commitment to achieving a noble desired condition that is good for everyone. Good leaders and followers work together to benefit everyone who depends on the organization as a whole, not just those with power who pursue narrow self-interest. Each organization has an actual and a potential capacity to select and support effective servant leadership that advances substantive change to achieve worthy desired conditions. Followers make the crucial difference because no one leads alone.

A person who does the work of leading helps the organization develop an adequately clear, consistent, and compelling vision of the future condition that the organization is setting out to achieve; provides a plausible plan of how you are going to get there; and by various means motivates enough organizational members to do what's necessary to move together to—or at least toward—that new place. There is a lot more to leading than this highly distilled essence, but there is not less.

Healthy and successful organizations are characterized by wise and effective followers who are able to identify the person whom they want to support in any given labor of leading. Wise and effective followers do not happen by accident in any organization. Healthy and successful organizations intentionally recruit members who demonstrate the humility and strength required to consistently practice this kind of active servant followership, and they intentionally invest in followership development for all members, including among those in positions of leadership. Such a culture of highly effective followership—starting with the board and C-level executives—attracts, develops, and retains the quality of leadership needed for organizational health and success in an unhealthy, competitive, but needy world.

If you want good leaders, you must have good followers. If you want morally good leaders who seek morally good outcomes that are truly good for everyone involved, you must have morally good followers. If you want truly great leaders, you must have truly great followers who know how to choose and support the right people to lead.

Follower Case: Better as My Friend Than My Leader

I like her and admire and trust her as a friend. She's very empathetic and we work together a lot at church on poverty programs. But she sometimes leads with her heart instead of her head, and her heart doesn't always listen to logic very well. So here, I don't think she fully understands how this industry really works, or what we need to be doing as a company to succeed. And she knows even less what all of us in my unit need from corporate leadership right now. Some of us are helping refine and explain the new salary plan, but we don't all support her big five-year vision. Personally, I'd like for her to succeed, but I sure don't see how her plan can afford the proposed compensation scales. A podcast I listened to made me seriously think that I need to be looking for another job, probably in a different company. Plus, I think it might help our friendship.

Meditation

Upright citizens are good for a city and make it prosper, but the talk of the wicked tears it apart.

. . . Without wise leadership a nation falls; there is safety in having many advisors. (Proverbs 11:11 and 14)

Whether the organization is a city, nation, business, church, government agency, family, or any other kind of organization, the character and quality of its "citizens" determine if it prospers or not. Wise and effective leadership is essential to organizational health and prosperity, and without it the organization fails. But strong and effective leadership ultimately depends on the full range of corporate wisdom that is centered in the primal power of strong and effective followership.

Talking with God

Gracious God, give every member of this organization a clear and correct understanding of the part they need to play in the collaboration of leading and following that will give us the wisdom and strength that we need for truly healthy and successful prosperity in the work of your Kingdom. Especially help me give my leaders what they need from me for them to succeed. With confident faith I thank you, and I commit to pray for my leaders and fellow followers. Amen.

Questions and Issues

A. If you are in a toxic organization that has a noble mission and good stated values, but has a board and/or CEO that is weak, uninformed, or compromised (e.g., by conflict of interest), how do you decide whether to stay and work for change or leave?

B. If you have a follower position, role, or personal preference, when and how do you decide that you need to do the work of leading in a certain situation?

C. What can you do to ensure that you make well-informed, objectively wise decisions about choosing and supporting a personal friend who wants a leadership position in an organization you both belong to, such as your employer, a school, your church, a political party, or local city or county government? How do you avoid both favoritism and overly scrupulous reservation for your friend as a leader or for yourself as a follower?

D. What makes attention to followership development so rare compared with all the attention given to leadership development?

E. What programs, if any, have you seen or experienced that were intentionally focused on improving the quality and/or effectiveness of followership?

CHAPTER 15

Every Type of Leadership Needs Its Corresponding Followership

Follower Case: Happy Follower

I am definitely a follower. I always have been. I think it fools people some-times that I am basically an extrovert. I love being with people, especially people who laugh a lot and kid around like me. I guess because I am gre-garious and kind of loud sometimes, and I share my views and opinions on things, I get asked to be in charge of things. My natural response is to say no, but then they usually seem glad when I say that I would help so-and-so if they could get them to lead it. Making people laugh and feel good and helping them get things done and done right—that is a lot more fun and satisfying for me than trying to make people do something I decided they have to do.

We need leaders, and the better they are at it, the better it is for every-one, but I think we mostly need a lot more happy, hard-working followers who get things done and have some fun in the process. I think I can usually tell who should lead, especially if they can listen to us but not blame us if they make a dumb decision. But I don't need to be the leader, and I don't think less of myself for being a follower. A lot of leaders don't seem very happy. I prefer ones who are.

When you understand the primal power of the followers to determine who leads them, the logic naturally requires that every type of leader needs its corresponding type of follower. Happy followers want a happy leader. A narcissistic leader needs followers who can resonate with narcissism. Lead-ing to preserve existing conditions, values, or beliefs depends on following

98

that prefers protecting the present vision to risks of changing for a different future vision. A leader who uses the organization (whether it is a nation or a nonprofit) to increase their personal wealth needs followers who support that organizational purpose, usually also for themselves. Followers who want to feel good favor an inspirational leader who assures them that they are succeeding and all is well, regardless of how things might look. Followers who are willing to sacrifice to achieve desired conditions in the world want a leader who will sacrifice with them and for them. A morally motivated leader needs morally motivated followers. An immoral leader needs followers who want the same moral latitude for themselves, or who will at least ignore the leader's immorality as a tradeoff for other desired conditions.

The relationship between leader and follower can take many forms, but to grasp this principle we need only to ponder the reality that leaders and followers always depend on each other and always influence each other. The variety of permutations and combinations of such relationships are endless, but the basic principle always prevails. "To have good leaders you have to have good followers" (David Brooks).[16]

David Brooks applies this principle to the process of selecting and empowering elected leaders in his insightful declaration about the necessity of good followers. In a democracy you need to choose leaders you can trust, because, for the duration of their term in office after they are elected, voters must defer to them until the next opportunity to vote for or against them. With so many voters holding such diverse perspectives on a huge array of issues, there is no good mechanism for ongoing accountability.

The implication is clear that, as good citizen-followers, voters must choose leaders wisely for the good of the whole organization, for the body politic as a whole, not just for a collection of special interests and favored groups of supporters. And then citizen-followers must actively and effectively work for the success of the leaders that get elected. The related implication is that citizen-followers must also actively work to limit the damage of those public officials who betray the trust of those they serve. True public servants who deserve the trust of their citizen-followers must be honored, protected, and supported by active followership. And those who do not serve well as leaders must be replaced with better leaders.

Thus, in close elections 49 percent of the voters may justifiably decide that the person who was elected with 51 percent of the votes is not truly their leader and that therefore they may think they have no obligation to support that person's leadership. They may even actively work to undermine or even demonize the leader. It is a conundrum that plagues many if not all the nation states that practice some form of democratic polity. The future of democracy as a form of government depends on the full engagement of wise, informed, and active citizen followership, including those who fill the role of the loyal opposition.

Followership matters immensely, not just in the election of public officials but in every kind of organization. Good leaders cannot prevail without the support of enough good followers. Unfortunately, the negative corollary is also true.

Bad leaders require bad followers.

Just as good leaders need enough good followers, bad leaders must have enough bad followers to maintain their leadership. The implications of this reality are so distasteful that most people prefer to simply reject the notion and seek some other explanation that absolves the followers. An example of this process is evident when citizens demonstrate after a presidential election with signs that say, "Not my president." That mindset does not change the reality that whoever gets elected is indeed your president or legislator or local official if you are a citizen. Nor does the disavowal remove the citizen-follower's responsibilities, including holding leaders accountable; it merely ignores reality. If enough concerned citizen-followers remove themselves from the process or actively seek to simply resist the leader in every possible way, the resulting polarization can help ensure organizational fragmentation and failure. Broken unhealthy organizations more easily attract broken, unhealthy, or incompetent leaders and allow them to rise and prosper.

Followers decide who leads and who succeeds by acting on their decisions about the ways they will support, question, resist, or abandon a person in a given leadership role. In *The Allure of Toxic Leaders*[17] Jean Lipman-Blumen explains why toxic leaders can so often attract strongly committed followers for support, even with lies and deceptions. The fault lies within the followers.

Susceptible followers give power to leaders who the followers believe will give them something they lack or protect them from something they fear. They grant leadership power on the expectation of satisfying such personal needs or desires. Their felt need may stem from an injured or uncertain sense of personal worth, prejudice against people who are different, fear of competition, a sense of group shame, or any of countless other sources. Such followers rationalize or simply choose to disregard factual truths and seek a leader who promises to change their world so they do not need to change themselves, including what they want to believe. Their choice of leader must make them look and feel smart, successful, and safe, rather than foolish, feckless, and vulnerable. They may fear that changing their mind indicates an original stupidity rather than mature wisdom. Toxic leaders fan smoldering insecurity and fear into a flame of disrespect and even hatred for fellow humans whom God created and loves. Toxic leaders must find and/or create sufficiently toxic followers. Healthy leaders must attract, strengthen, and inspire healthy followership.

One of the best-known, large-scale, and convincing examples of this principle is World War II in Europe. Hitler and Churchill were strong and effective leaders of two great nations that faced each other in war. History judges Hitler to have led his nation to commit morally heinous atrocities in an effort to blame, denigrate, expel, or kill people that they believed caused their humiliating economic distress after World War I and thus should rightly be hated and punished as enemies. Some of these hated enemies were fellow German citizens and others were the people of other nations. Christian churches generally supported or silently accepted Hitler's fanning the flames of fear and hatred.

Churchill is honored for leading his beleaguered nation to the moral high ground and the successful defense of human freedom and the worth of all people. Both men were effective leaders who mobilized their nations to significant achievements. Both of them used persuasion, power, and alliances to accomplish their purposes. Most leaders do. Those who want to claim that Churchill was a real leader and Hitler was not really a leader are simply trying to narrow the concept of leadership to fit their theory or ideal type. But doing so leads to logical dead ends.

You may judge that Hitler was not a desirable or morally acceptable leader, but that does not mean he was not an effective leader who moved an entire nation, and in some ways the world, to a dramatically new condition. He was supported by enough active followers who wanted him to succeed for their own benefit, plus enough additional passive followers who decided not to resist, in hopes of getting specifically defined outcomes that they wanted. If the bad followers supported a bad leader partly in ignorance or apathy, that fact does not exempt them but simply clarifies what kind of bad followers

they were. At that time Germany had enough anti-Semitism, enough toler-
ance of violence and brutality by political parties, and enough injured chau-
vinistic pride, along with other elements of their national psyche, that Hitler
could exploit the conditions of external oppression, economic chaos, and political fragmentation to become the ruthless dictator of the Third Reich. His
title was *fuhrer,* leader.

The allure that attracts followers to toxic, unhealthy leaders comes from
within the followers, from the followers' own unhealthy desires and fears that
they want to believe are good. Toxic leaders can only rise and prevail with the
support or acquiescence of enough toxic followers. Followers tend to choose
and support leaders to fit the extrapolated image of their own idealized self.
Leaders in turn help shape their followers' self-perception and desires, which
ultimately determines who leads and toward what organizational character
and desired conditions. From godly to ghastly, every type of leadership needs
its corresponding followership.

Meditation

> Finally, all the elders of Israel met at Ramah to discuss the matter
> with Samuel. . . . Give us a king to judge us like all the other na-
> tions have. Samuel was displeased with their request and went to
> the Lord for guidance. "Do everything they say to you," the Lord
> replied, "for it is me they are rejecting, not you. They don't want
> me to be their king any longer. . . . Do as they ask, but solemnly
> warn them about the way a king will reign over them."
>
> . . . But the people refused to listen to Samuel's warning. "Even
> so, we still want a king," they said. "We want to be like the nations
> around us." . . . Then Samuel agreed and sent the people home. (I
> Samuel 8:4-21)

Whether the organization is a city, nation, business, church, government agency, family, or any other kind of organization, the character and
quality of its "citizens" determine if it prospers or not. The people of Israel
had a unique opportunity to have God as their king and be the Kingdom
of God on earth. Instead, they wanted a visible king like the nations around
them. In his grace and forbearance God blessed them with good leadership from some human kings. But more commonly they chose and suffered
under unhealthy and ineffective human leaders. Wise and effective leader-

ship is essential to organizational health and prosperity, and without it the organization suffers and eventually fails. But strong and effective leadership ultimately depends on the full range of corporate wisdom that is centered in strong, effective, and wise followership.

Talking with God

Gracious God, give every member of this organization a clear and correct understanding of themselves, and the part they need to play in the identification of leaders. Help us learn from each other how to practice the collaboration of leading and following that will give us the wisdom and strength that we need for truly healthy and successful prosperity in the work of your Kingdom. With confident faith I pray for us, and I thank you for redeeming our errors in this process. Amen.

Questions and Issues

A. How do you make the Kingdom of God your highest priority when you are an involuntary follower of elected governmental leader(s) whom you voted against or organizational leaders whose values and/or vision you think are wrong? What deference or respect, if any, is appropriately due to them? What is appropriate in the opposite case when your preferred leader has power over others who are not "happy followers"?

B. What are some ways that you can appropriately and effectively work for wise public policies or organizational policies that you believe align with the Kingdom for the good of everyone, including in particular those who have no faith in God?

C. How can you intentionally guard yourself against inadvertently supporting a toxic leader because they are similar to you or they support something that you believe is good and important?

D. God is sovereign and uses all kinds of earthly people and events to achieve his ultimate purposes and fully establish his Kingdom under Jesus Christ. Why should you try to seek first the Kingdom of God if all things ultimately work together for our good and his glory anyway?

The Great Distinction in Leadership

When the governing board of Fresno Pacific engaged with me about becoming the chief executive officer, they were overtly looking for a president to whom they could safely delegate their responsibility for leading and managing with formal control over the affairs of the organization according to their policies and missional directives and in compliance with applicable laws. The board members believed firmly and correctly that organizational success depends on effective leadership and management for the particular situation. They understood that the single most important responsibility of a governing board is the selection, direction, and evaluation of the president.

The board knew that moving to a new and very different future would never happen by some happy accident of organizational drift in the right direction. The kind of transformational change that they had previously approved and were working to advance needed to be intentional. A certain kind of leadership process is required to create a different organizational culture and vision while respecting the enduring beliefs, mission, core values, and essential relationships for which the organization exists.

The board needed to ensure that their authority and power as a governing board would be used to fulfill their legal responsibilities and satisfy their spiritual intentions for a healthy and successful institution that effectively served the Kingdom of God. Their role was to govern and guide the institution to certain specific desired conditions. They did not exist to manage or administer its affairs. They needed to fill the position of president with a person to whom they could delegate their authority and power to direct the activities of all the employees so that they would be an institution that produced certain outcomes. They needed a president who could lead by effectively using the available organizational power for organizational transformation.

But in their hearts they knew that they also needed a president whom people inside and outside the organization would willingly follow, inform, protect, and support through all the tough changes that would be needed for the institution to transform itself under challenging circumstances. They needed a president who also could lead without using the available organizational power. Leading with power and leading without power would both be important, but first they had to properly arrange the power structure of the organization. They had to ensure that the foundation of leading with organizational power was solidly laid with a president who had power and the authority to use it.

What the Fresno Pacific Board and the employees and I sensed intuitively, but did not fully and overtly understand as we were going through the process together, was the great distinction between these two kinds of leading and their complementary patterns of following. We did not adequately and consciously appreciate the great differences between leading with power over people and leading without such power. We dealt with this complicated reality instinctively and reactively, taking disjointed and sometimes inconsistent actions or using contradictory language that often had to be corrected to get things right. We discussed, discerned, prayed, agonized, and argued together. In our disagreements we often displayed and observed the passive-aggressive patterns that are prevalent in many kinds of organizations, but which certain religious faith traditions refine to a high art, complete with theological rhetoric that feels irresistible.

Secular organizations can easily commit their version of the same blunders because of the same kind of blindness that obscures the obvious. We would have benefited greatly from a richer understanding of leadership with and without such power and the nature and responsibility of our followership in these two different contexts. We could have done it all much better if we had understood the two kinds of leading more completely, respected them more openly, and referenced them more explicitly. As we bumped into it or stumbled over it, we made pragmatic decisions, but our obvious reality was too often invisible to us and thus remained unreferenced. The great distinction in leadership was invisible to us, so our interdependent following was too often inefficient or ineffective.

It is attractive to avoid all that complexity, but doing so leaves us with organizations that do not perform as well as they could. What is needed is what Oliver Wendel Holmes is credited with calling the simplicity on the other side of the complexity, and in organizational life, the resulting deeper simplicity will always acknowledge the great distinction between leading with power and leading without power. The central issue is the capacity to make things happen in the world, but sometimes what seems obvious as conventional wisdom simply is not the whole truth. And sometimes what appears to be less is really more, and what seems slower is really the faster— or even the only—path to the desired conditions.

The prophetic judgment that the board of Fresno Pacific had to make at that critical juncture was whether there would be sufficient followership for their presidential appointee to actually lead the change process that they wanted. To many of them the presidential selection felt like nothing more than a hunch, a hopeful and prayerful shot in the dark. In many ways I was not an ideal candidate. Some people were convinced that I was not even an adequate candidate. I lacked the normal managerial and leadership experience, having never been a cabinet level corporate manager. I did not have any history or identity with the sponsoring denomination. I was relatively new to the organization and its constituencies, and I was new to the primary market region and its amalgamation of highly diverse cultures.

Hope is the child of faith.

The board had to determine from their collective wisdom whether they could reasonably expect enough people to follow me so that I would have some hope of succeeding as the president. For some board members it was one of those situations where necessity is the mother of hope. For others hope was the child of faith. But for all of them together as a governing board, just as for most decision-making bodies that face such choices, to make the right leadership selection with any consistency depends on understanding—or simply sensing by practical intuition—the great leadership distinction. They needed someone who would be able to lead without exercising hierarchical power but who would also lead by invoking executive power when needed.

Because formal positional leaders are readily identifiable and obviously visible, they are understandably viewed as uniquely or independently important people in an organization, and they are recognized and rewarded accordingly. Leadership is the process that receives all the attention, and leading is the activity that really matters to everyone. Preoccupation with leadership can become so pervasive that ultimately everyone in the organization is called a leader, and everyone is supposed to be leading all the time. But that approach naturally produces an interesting final condition. If everyone is supposed to be a leader all the time, who is following? And if nobody is following, then no one is really leading, either with power or without power, because, by definition, a leader has followers, and followers create a leader when they accept that person's influence in their lives and act on it.

To understand this principle, we need an adequate concept of followership. Although the field of followership has a much shorter history and a much smaller body of literature than the field of leadership, diverse definitions of followership have proliferated. Underneath all of them is one universal, comprehensible, and unarguable definition of a follower, a definition that is true for every kind of follower in every followership situation.

The great distinction in leadership is not a new idea. Amitai Etzioni developed this concept as early as 1964 when he complicated the tidy world of what is called "scientific management" by explaining the distinction between what he called formal and informal leadership in organizations. "The importance of leadership for setting and enforcing group norms and the difference between informal and formal leadership constitutes another major modification of scientific management."[18] Etzioni proposed that the school of scientific management tends to view the organization as a formal entity based primarily on transactional agreements. The employees are paid to perform certain tasks or achieve certain results for the organization.

By contrast, the school of human relations sought a balance or accommodation between the organization's goals and the goals and interests of the employees. He contended that organizations demonstrate the existence of both models simultaneously. He saw these as "the concepts of formal and informal organization" coexisting in a dynamic, complex, and interactive reality in organizations as diverse as factories, churches, prisons, and schools. Every kind of formal organization with formal positional leadership also has an informal organization with informal personal leadership.[19]

In describing the great distinction between formal positional leadership and informal personal leadership, Etzioni explored the interaction of these two types of leadership in the conceptual contexts of two different approaches or schools of thought: scientific management and human relations.

He primarily used data and insights on secular, for-profit corporations. But the case of Fresno Pacific University confirms that the same structural and social dynamics operate in a religious nonprofit organizational environment. In fact, these principles are so fundamental that they apply in some fashion to organizations of every possible configuration that seek every possible kind of purpose and espouse every conceivable set of beliefs, values, and behaviors.

From the smallest church or nonprofit service organization to the largest government agency, multinational corporation, sovereign nation, or volunteer movement, the leadership process displays some version of the great distinction between formal and informal leadership and followership.

Leading as the formal superordinate with managerial power over people who are subordinates in a hierarchical structure of positions with defined responsibilities and authorities is the most common and most visible pattern of working relationships in organizations. This typical pattern includes paid employees laboring at the unforgiving demands of producing a financial surplus that will sustain the organization. Leading without power is typically more prevalent among people serving as unpaid staff or group members, typically in not-for-profit or religious organizations.

However, this generalization tends to obscure the power-based relationships and activities in nonprofit, volunteer, or religious organizations, just as it obscures the significant reality of voluntary relationships and activities in for-profit and governmental agencies with paid and intentionally managed employees. Increasingly the best public benefit organizations look and feel like high performing for-profits, and—especially in the digital internet world—the for-profits function and feel a lot like not-for-profits.

Both modes of leadership are important, and both depend on the primal power of followership. In either mode, the followers determine who leads them, where they are willing to go, and what they are willing to do to get there.

Meditation

Jesus and his companions went to the town of Capernaum. When the Sabbath day came, he went into the synagogue and began to teach. The people were amazed at his teaching, for he taught with real authority—quite unlike the teachers of religious law. Suddenly a man in the synagogue who was possessed by an evil spirit began shouting, "Why are you interfering with us Jesus of Nazareth? Have you come to destroy us? I know who you are—the Holy One sent from God!"

Jesus cut him short. "Be quiet! Come out of the man," he ordered. At that, the evil spirit screamed, threw the man into a convulsion, and then came out of him. Amazement gripped the audience, and they began to discuss what had happened. "What sort of new teaching is this?" they asked excitedly. "It has such authority! Even evil spirits obey his orders!" The news about Jesus spread quickly. (Mark 1:21-28)

Jesus, Son of God, sinless Son of Man, and King over all creation, had all authority and power at his command. The evil spirit unwillingly accepted the reality that Jesus had power over him. The people in the synagogue recognized the unique authority they sensed when Jesus taught them, a compelling authority they realized was completely different from the authority of their religious leaders. He invited them to believe and follow him, but all the text says is that they marveled. It does not say that they granted him influence in their lives and followed him.

He could have led with invincible power, full knowledge, and perfect decisions to immediately establish his glorious Kingdom on earth just as his followers hoped he would. But to achieve his longer vision and greater purpose, he taught and modeled how to lead without power. He came to earth to demonstrate God's love and invite people to freely choose to follow him in his Kingdom. Imperfect human organizations, including the Church, use both kinds of leadership—with and without invoking managerial power—but always with a firm foundation in servant followership.

Jesus demonstrates leading with power and leading without power. He claimed and demonstrated his enormous authority on earth with power to heal the sick and disabled, to raise the dead back to life, and to forgive sins. He also led with power by telling his disciples what to do when he sent them out to experience the rising power of the Kingdom of God on earth. But, although he announced the coming of God's kingdom on earth and presented himself as the one true King with mighty armies of angels under his command and power over evil, he sought voluntary followership and led his earthly followers without exercising monarchial leadership power over their actions.

Jesus exercised power directly to overcome the power of the Evil One. And he also delegated his kingdom authority and power to his inner circle of voluntary followers for whom he modeled leading with the humble heart of a servant. His first coming allows people to freely choose to accept God's loving forgiveness. When he comes again, he will establish and lead his kingdom with absolute and perfect power.

Talking with God

Heavenly Father, as I try to advance your Kingdom on earth it is so easy for me to get it wrong when I am deciding whether to lead with organizational power, lead without invoking that power, or lead with some combination of them—or even follow someone else. And even when I choose the right mode of leadership or followership, I am frustratingly vulnerable to error in trying to do it, especially when I forget to pause and ask for the wisdom of your Holy Spirit to protect my followers from my leadership flaws and my leaders from my flawed followership. In the name of Jesus I ask for wisdom in the work of your Kingdom. Amen.

Questions and Issues

A. What are examples of being moved to action by someone who was leading without power? Leading with power? What caused action in each case?

B. What is the key to effective leading without power when the leader does have formal leadership authority over the subordinates that could be invoked?

C. What is the best way for a follower to indicate that they need the leader to switch from leading without power to leading with power, or the reverse?

D. Jesus claimed to have "all authority." Did he use both kinds of leading? Examples? Was working miracles a way to lead with power or without power?

E. How is trust different in leading with power and leading without power?

Leadership Is
Simply Complicated

L eadership is complicated, not just in the sense that *in practice* leadership often involves high risk actions under conditions of uncertainty with no second chances or do-overs. Leadership is also complicated because leadership—as a word, a concept, a practice, a process, and a set of principles—is plagued by multiple definitions and unresolved contradictions.

One person's great leader may be someone else's evil tyrant, while a third person sees no real leader at all, just a manger with no human empathy. Bernard Bass identified and developed hundreds of concepts, definitions, analytical frameworks, operational approaches, typologies, taxonomies, classifications, theories, styles, patterns, and models of leadership.[20] Joseph Rost identified 221 definitions of leadership that he found in 587 books, book chapters, and journal articles with the word leadership in the title, starting in the 1920s when the earliest such books appeared and running through 1990. Just as enlightening is the fact that the other 366 sources that Rost found on leadership explored the subject of leadership without even trying to define it.[21]

The high priority of efforts to improve leadership continues to support the ongoing proliferation of books, dissertations, articles, seminars, webinars, blogs, foundations, institutes, and countless other sources of wisdom on leadership, management, and organizational effectiveness. The total body of such sources has continued to multiply, with each expert adding their particular perspective on what leadership really is and how it should be practiced and evaluated. Leadership is what people in leadership positions or roles contribute to organizational outcomes, but leadership is also a process, and it is the result of that process. Some concepts of leadership recognize that without followership there is no leadership, but the focus remains on leadership.

Even if you accept the simplest working definitions—that a leader has followers and a follower has chosen a leader—there is no comprehensive and universally accepted framework for considering all the different phenomena that comprise the field. A diverse set of sincere truth seekers must use the same words with different meanings, nuances, and modifiers to deal with the unresolved dilemmas, ambiguities, contradictions, impasses, lacunae, and confusions around the critical but complicated field of following and leading.

Truth and effectiveness get lost when words lose their clear and consistent meaning.

Sometimes the loss of the truth about following and leading is intentional, but more commonly in the field of leadership and organizational behavior it is the inadvertent result of an accumulation of skillful and well-intended efforts to explain and improve leadership, whatever it is. The inconsistent and sometimes erroneous use of concepts and language has made leadership and followership difficult to study or even to simply discuss. Terms and distinctions that are essential to understanding each other as leaders and as followers need adequate working definitions that are consistently understood and applied. The principles of followership must be viewed as being just as important for organizational success as leadership principles, and the development of more powerful and effective followers must be valued as an essential element in understanding and improving the collaborative process of leading and following in organizational performance.

One common and helpful response to the challenge of understanding leadership is to contextualize the leadership and followership words by adding modifiers that differentiate the various kinds, types, or ways of leading and the different kinds of leaders. We talk about administrative leadership, military leadership, spiritual leadership, visionary leadership, transformational leadership, transactional leadership, political leadership, intellectual leadership, strategic leadership, tactical leadership, academic leadership, religious leadership, leadership of a movement or cause, leadership as the first one to act, servant leadership, steward leadership, and hundreds of other such leaderships and followerships. All these variations can help in a particular situation, but they still leave unresolved the need for consistency in a larger and more comprehensive framework.

Even when you do contextualize and otherwise differentiate the many kinds of leaders and leadership and their related forms of following, the tendency to miscommunicate and misunderstand too often leads to blunders in ways that make a negative difference in organizational performance and thus in people's lives. Creating hundreds of different leaderships enriches the narrative but does not eliminate the underlying problems of misunderstandings and inefficiencies.

The confusion is actually even deeper and more complex than it appears, because all these types of leadership and leaders vary qualitatively. Each type of leader and follower can be effective or ineffective, morally good or bad, loved or despised, a success or a failure, wise or foolish, altruistic or self-centered, empathetic, sympathetic, or simply pathetic.

Find the simplicity on the other side of the complexity.

Warren Bennis says that "leadership is like beauty: it's hard to define, but you know it when you see it."[22] However, that is not to say that leadership is always beautiful, only that you can recognize authentic and effective leadership by seeing the process or the results, which can range from delightful to dreadful. Followership defines leadership but followership is harder to notice and even harder to recognize.

Ideally, a leader has sufficient informal or personal influence, in addition to the formal power of an organizational titled executive position, to provide a wide spectrum of leadership effectiveness, and also move fluidly into the role and functions of effective followership. There is a wide range of combinations on a continuum from leaders with no informal personal power to leaders with little or no formal positional power, and some who follow effectively, while others struggle and stumble trying to follow and support other leaders. Competency for any mode of leadership is learned; "leaders are made, not born," and the most effective follower-leaders are those who continue "to grow and develop throughout life."[23]

Ignoring or misunderstanding the great distinction between leading *with* power and *without* power are common in most organizations, along with the deep habit of ignoring the primal power of followership in both modes of leadership. The price of this ignorance is evidenced in countless ways, including: contradictory expectations, inefficiency, ineffectiveness, miscommunication, confusion, frustration, blaming, low levels of trust, low satisfaction among group members, and dissatisfied customers, clients, and other publics. Confounding two other key words exacerbates the problem. Management and administration are two different modes of organizational operation. All these differences matter.

Thus, a comprehensive schema of organizational theory and praxis needs to include the different kinds of leading and following that determine how effective an organization is at being healthy for people and financially successful. It all rests on the same conceptual and semantic framework. There are two core modes of leading—leading with power and leading without power—and two core modes of action or implementation—management and administration. And there is a corresponding array of distinguishing elements and modes of followership that are required to support and sustain the variations and combinations of leadership, management, and administration.

The level of effectiveness on every organizational effort, event, or process depends on getting the right people doing the right things in the right way. It depends on the right leadership supported by the necessary followership. Using a shared conceptual framework helps everyone involved to see who and what is needed—and not needed—to get any particular job done properly. The comprehensive array of those elements of leading and following can be called an Effectiveness Framework. (See one model on page 135.) You can create one that works for your whole organization, from which you select what is needed for each key event or process. This approach can help give an organization a stable and spacious conceptual field within which all the nuances can be framed and misunderstandings can at least be minimized to ensure achievement of each key indicator.

Such a framework for concepts and terminology needs to be wisely, creatively, and consistently developed, discussed, and applied for each relevant aspect of organizational life. But that good intention is easily and often jeopardized by the fact that leadership looks and acts and feels so different in different situations, and that followership is often misconstrued or simply ignored, instead of being recognized, improved, and fully engaged.

Although there is no exhaustive compendium of all the concepts or definitions of leadership, it is useful to consider a suggestive or representative list of some of the common concepts that have simply endured, with the note that there is some element of utility in almost every one of the hundreds of concepts of organizational leadership. The following are simply examples from the complicated set of different concepts of what leadership is. Behaviors or actions that contribute to organizational success:

1. Whatever leaders do (whether right or wrong)
2. Inducing compliance (by whatever means)
3. Excellent management
4. Special engagement with the world
5. Exercise of influence—either unidirectional or mutually interactive
6. Use of power or management in human systems or relationships
7. Management of organizational or system structure
8. Values infusion
9. A particular form or expression of servanthood
10. Self-expression
11. Persuasive communication
12. Person or process that enables organizational goal achievement
13. Personality type
14. Exercise of a particular set of valued personal characteristics
15. Agent, initiator, or process of change
16. Relationship between leader and follower
17. Obtaining and exercising power over other persons
18. Personification of the organization
19. Differentiated role in a social system
20. Influence of any kind on some other person's thoughts, feelings, or action

There are many other definitions. Each view of leaders, leading, or leadership has proven useful, and each can contribute to a more adequate and accurate understanding of some specific organizational situation or process. Many different types or categories of leadership depend on the outcomes, emphasis, values, personal styles, personalities, or risks that are part of an organizational situation or setting.

The term leadership, used as a noun, is more complicated to define than the word leader, and it includes at least two closely related meanings. Leadership is the process that involves a leader and followers working purposefully together to achieve some desired result. Leadership is also what leaders do as part of that leadership process. This aspect of leadership as a relational process supports the ongoing effort to understand and work with the traits or characteristics of leaders, and of varying styles of leadership. Such elements are important factors in how people decide whether or not to follow and support a particular leader.

Modified by an adjective, the term leadership is used in countless different combinations with appropriately nuanced meanings for each situation. There is no good alternative to using the word leadership in all these varied ways, and no great mischief results, provided that the underlying concepts of the critical terms are clarified and respected.

The following descriptors are an illustrative sample of the countless ways you can modify a definition or concept of leader, leading, and leadership in attempting to make sense of them and use the one that fits a particular position or situation. The following items present a range of examples, but it is not an attempt to be exhaustive. You combine any definition of what leadership is with one or more of the ways you can indicate a more specific kind or type of that leadership.

1. Transactional
2. Transformational
3. Collaborative
4. Dictatorial/autocratic/tyrannical
5. Educational
6. Inclusive
7. Intellectual or thought
8. Managerial
9. Religious
10. Military
11. Process oriented

12. Results oriented

13. Hereditary/inherited

14. Spiritual

15. Strategic

16. Governmental

17. Turnaround

18. Positional

19. Charismatic

20. Political

21. Participative

22. Administrative

23. Legislative

24. Steward

25. Prophetic

26. Situational

27. Media-based

Obviously, these illustrative lists of definitions and kinds or types of leaders or leadership could be significantly expanded, but it demonstrates the great potential for misunderstanding across all these variables when people try to communicate about a person or process with differing assumptions about what it is or which particular kind it is. To simply frame one interesting pair as an example: you sense significant differences between political leadership and spiritual leadership, even though we know that many political leaders are truly guided by spiritual values, and that others allude to them. We also know that spiritual leaders often have to deal with thorny political issues in their formal organizations or informal ideological movements.

Nevertheless, a political leader or a passionately partisan follower refers to something quite different from a spiritual leader or a sacrificially devout and dedicated religious follower. You can intuitively sense the commonalities in these two types of leading and following, but you also sense the huge differences. Confounding these concepts invites political leaders to mislead by feigning false spirituality, as it tempts religious leaders to seek and abuse political power.

It is no surprise that common usage settled for the simplicity on the near side of the true complexity of leading and following in the attempt to develop healthy and successful organizations. The greater challenge is to discover and apply the simplicity on the far side of messy organizational reality, the simplicity that frames, structures, and explicates the meanings that are latent in the apparent chaos. From the other side leading and following can look quite different. The language, logic, and actions of the leadership process make a real difference in the lives of many real people.

Meditation

"Always be full of joy in the Lord. I say it again—rejoice! Let everyone see that you are considerate in all you do. Remember, the Lord is coming soon." (Phil 4:4-5)

God gives a certain joy in our relationship with him when we consider what is good for everyone who is affected by something that really matters. The Lord feels present when we are sincerely committed to understanding other perspectives and respecting people that we think are not seeing it correctly. That consideration creates complexity that is usually more confusing and uncomfortable than our initial condition of unexplored differences, but it is the path to the simplicity of actionable consensus on the other side of the confusing complexity. And it is preparation for the coming of the Lord's peace and prosperity now and when the Kingdom is fully realized.

Talking with God

Gracious God, let every member of this organization experience the gift of your joy as we seek together a clear and correct understanding of the part each one needs to play in choosing whom to follow and finding consensus in all the confusion. Give us the wisdom and strength that we need for truly healthy and successful work in your Kingdom. Give each of us the humility to see and understand what some of us can see but is invisible or confusing to others. With confident faith I thank you for the light of your Spirit guiding us through the darkness of our shared confusion to a shared vision. Amen.

Questions and Issues

A. Does it work for you to define and discuss leadership in terms of followers who accept someone's influence in their thinking? Give an explanatory example, either pro or con.

B. What should we infer about leadership from the fact that Jesus did not tell us to lead? He certainly knew that organizational leading would happen as his followers implemented his commission to go and make disciples who trust the King and seek the Kingdom. But he taught them to focus on loving and serving, not on becoming powerful leaders. What does this tell us about leading and following?

C. How will organizational leading and following be different or remain the same as it is now in the visible Kingdom of God that will be fully realized under the sovereign authority of the King, Jesus Christ?

D. How do you experience "joy in the Lord" and being "considerate in all you do" if you work in or engage with organizations that do not recognize or practice kingdom values? What are your options if they formally reject or actively contradict these and other kingdom values as you understand them?

PART 3

Doing
Effectiveness

CHAPTER 18

Know What You Are Doing

Do you know what you're doing?" My Dad would ask me that effectiveness question without any pejorative intent. What condition would exist from my activity? What would it take to make that result happen? Sometimes he would help me reconceptualize my activity by describing it as a different final result. I was not just painting a wall of our house; I was making Mom very happy and also increasing the beauty and the value of our house, while also mastering a valuable skill that I could use all my life, including making money. And each of those results was pleasing to God. Knowing what you are really doing is important. Effectiveness is intentionally achieving a particular effect, a desired condition, a defined outcome. Effectiveness is something you do to produce an effect.

When achieving the desired condition requires organized activity by more than one person, shared understanding is essential. You need to know what matters and why, and who is doing what to coordinate activity and get the desired organizational effectiveness. Efficiency is effectiveness with the least resources. So, efficiency is often—but not always—part of "the right way" to do something with minimum waste. In some cases efficiency is just as important as effectiveness and it may even become the effective goal. In some cases achieving the effect is all that matters.

An Effectiveness Framework provides a simplified, unified, and comprehensive conceptual structure that allows all participants in any organizational process to analyze what they are doing, why it matters, who is following whom, and what following and leading is needed to get the desired effect. (See an example on page 103.) Such a framework helps ensure a shared understanding of the elements of effective following and leading that will be required to achieve the desired condition.

123

This planning tool recognizes four macro-types or modes of leading: with power, without power, managerial, and administrative. It helps everyone involved understand and communicate about the major elements of any situation. It is *not* a detailed project management system, but it helps you create and evaluate such tools, especially if there are uncontrollable factors, such as people with new assignments, indications of uncertainty about leadership capacity or followership support, or critical things that might not go as well as they need to.

- What am I and the other key players really trying to accomplish? What main role does each person or group need to play?

- What is the most important contribution that I and other key players need to make?

- Is any key person, relationship, or other component missing or inadequate?

- What do I and other key players need from each other to be effective and successful in making the most important contributions to the effort?

- What consistent meanings and assumptions are needed for effectiveness?

A comprehensive conceptualization of effectiveness builds on the core concept of organizational roles and functions. A role constitutes a connected set of capacities and characteristics that contributes a valuable effect for the team. Normally every formal position with a title and authority in the organizational hierarchy includes one or more role definition, plus specified functions and related authority. Throughout his *Followership* book Atchison calls the people in such positions "titled executives," because they may or may not really be effective leaders.[24] They range on a continuum from strong and effective to weak and ineffective. A "weak, titled executive" is, by definition, not really a leader. But informal personal roles also make a big difference, and those informal roles do not depend on any particular organizational position or title. For example, a chief operations officer has a position description and the authority to make certain decisions, but the person with that title may or may not have the empathy or listening skills required for the role of consoling and encouraging people after a failure, loss, or tragedy. An Effectiveness Framework helps everyone see what is needed, who could do it, who will do it, and what support they will need to achieve the desired condition.

One of the easiest ways to understand formal and informal organizational roles is in team sports, where players may play particular roles in addition to their assigned position. A player may have a special knack of doing or saying something that inspires hope when things are going badly. A player may have a habit of making a key defensive stop and turning it into a scoring opportunity. Someone may have an uncanny knack of anticipating what will happen and ensuring that the right team members also see it.

For anyone to effectively play a leadership role, whether formal or informal, followers must accept that person in that role for the given situation. Every leadership event and experience is shaped for any particular follower by where the follower experiences it on the continuum from coercion through obligation to enthusiastic voluntarism.

Trust among leaders and followers is a factor in each of the four leadership modes. Integrity means people can safely depend on you to perform as expected. The trust may be earned by demonstrated consistency of effectiveness, or the trust may be imputed by logical analysis, such as when a person has some recognized credential or other qualification. The trust may be positional trust (e.g., they have the right title and authority), or it may be simple blind trust in the absence of any better alternative. The strongest trust and followership are rightly assumed to be a product of voluntarily choosing to believe in and trust the integrity of a leader.

Trust is a child of integrity.

An Effectiveness Framework recognizes the factors that define and distinguish the four main modes of organizational leadership.

A. Lead without power: Any member of the organization can make someone their personal or informal leader by choosing to accept that person's influence in their lives and by committing themselves to enhance the effectiveness of that leader for the follower's own interests and, ideally, also for the success of the whole organization. Informal influence is vested in the leader by the followers.

125

A personal leader has influence that is accepted by those members of the organization who trust the leader to know and do what is right for the future of the organization. Personal leadership is supported by voluntary personal followership within a system of relational influences that may or may not relate to any particular managerial structure, formal position, or organizational goal.

You cannot normally hire this kind of informal influential leader because you cannot control or know in advance who in the organization will and will not make voluntary decisions to accept their influence and help them succeed in their leadership role. But you do need to understand and act on accurate notions about the personal, informal leadership of any person (or group) that is significantly involved in the character, decisions, values, and performance of the organization.

B. Lead with power: Certain members of the organization can exercise their legal or corporate authority to officially make someone a positional or titled leader by giving them formal organizational power with the authority to exercise that power to achieve certain organizational purposes and goals. Formal power and authority are vested in the position, regardless of who fills the position.

A positional leader has defined power over the people, policies, and resources of the organization for the purpose of achieving certain conditions that the organization desires for its future. Positional leadership is supported by obligatory positional followership within a managerial or administrative structure.

You can hire this kind of positional leader for an organization because everyone who wants their own position in the organization is obligated to respect all the other positions of power in the organization's formal hierarchy. The followership that supports a position with leadership power is obligatory, not voluntary. The right to exercise formal positional power affects the balance of power and the options among the participants in any process.

C. Manage: Management is the set of people in titled organizational positions who are authorized to lead with power to achieve the goals and objectives that are the measurable indicators of organizational success. Management is also the term that refers to the work that managers do. A manager obtains and organizes the necessary resources and people to achieve the goals and objectives that make the mission, vision, purposes, values, policies, and plans of the organization an economically sustainable reality.

D. Administer: Administration is the particular form of managerial leading with power that is charged with ensuring that all relevant laws and regulations, agency requirements, and organizational policies, principles, and standards are properly applied, administered, and satisfied in the process of achieving the organizational mission, vision, purposes, values, and operational goals, objectives, and desired conditions. Persons with administrative authority may often be involved in the process of shaping organizational plans and policies, but they do so from the perspective of someone who will be responsible for safeguarding the legality and propriety of every organizational activity.

Followership permeates any system of organizing human activity for goal effectiveness. Every effective organizational leadership role should involve a large proportion of time and energy doing the work of followership. Most people in an organization operate in followership mode most of the time in most organizational situations and relationships, including those persons in formal leadership positions. In a healthy and successful organization everyone is trying to achieve excellent personal and work-team performance in a way that also helps everyone else and all other work-teams be more effective at what they are expected to accomplish. Each member of the organization needs to understand the difference between a position and a role.

Particular types of effective followership are required to support and strengthen the effectiveness of each leadership mode. By definition, without followership there is no leadership, and by extension of the definition, the quality of the followership largely determines the quality of leadership in an organization. In addition to determining who the actual leaders are, people doing the work of followership largely determine how successful the leadership people and processes are. One of the most important contributions of effective following is to help moderate and integrate the unavoidable conflict among the competing priorities and interests of the different modes and challenges of leadership. Wise and effective followership facilitates the ongoing search for the corporate wisdom that marks a healthy and successful organization that is advancing its alignment with the character and values of the Kingdom of God.

Meditation

> So when the apostles were with Jesus, they kept asking him, "Lord, has the time come for you to free Israel and restore our kingdom?"
>
> He replied, "The Father alone has the authority to set those dates and times, and they are not for you to know. But you will receive power when the Holy Spirit comes upon you. And you will be my witnesses, telling people about me everywhere—in Jerusalem, throughout Judea, in Samaria, and to the ends of the earth." (Acts 1:6-8)

Despite three years of consistent and creative explanations regarding the true nature of the Kingdom that Jesus was announcing and inaugurating, and especially its spiritual, voluntary, and inclusive character, Jesus' disciples did not understand what he was doing or what they should be doing. They misunderstood the kind of kingdom they were seeking, what kind of leadership Jesus was providing, and what type and degree of followership they needed to exercise. They persisted in thinking that they were engaged in the immediate establishment of a visible kingdom that Jesus would lead as a king with unlimited temporal power. Jesus does not tell them that such a glorious physical kingdom will never happen, because that time will eventually come, but with patient persistence he describes what they are doing right now and until further notice. Relying on spiritual power—not physical or political power—the task of Jesus-followers is to be witnesses who tell people everywhere about who Jesus really is. They will share the Good News that the Messiah-Savior-King has come and that through him God is forgiving and reconciling himself with anyone who voluntarily accepts Jesus as their Savior and follows him as their sovereign King. The disciples had the wrong vision of both the present and the future.

It helps to know what you are really doing and to understand how your efforts contribute to what all the other leading and following and organizing is trying to accomplish. The members of the visible kingdom that King Jesus will lead with absolute power in the future will be all those people who freely choose now by faith to follow the invisible king of a spiritual kingdom. The power of Jesus' followers during the present period of extended kingdom recruitment will be the power of the Holy Spirit, not the political power that overthrows the Roman or any other earthly political power. The highest priority in every area of life for his followers is to participate in building the spiritual kingdom that eventually becomes the gloriously visible Kingdom of God on earth as it is in heaven.

Making the Kingdom of God your guiding ideal and model of organizational life on earth now requires understanding how each mode of effective leadership ultimately depends on its corresponding form of effective followership. Every person and every organizational role matters in the Kingdom of God, and their interdependence must characterize and advance the corporate wisdom that produces constant change toward an organization in the Kingdom of God. When Jesus came to earth the first time as Savior and Messiah, he demonstrated his power over evil, but he led his followers without invoking power over them. When Jesus returns to earth as sovereign King, it will be different. He will lead with absolute power and perfection over his whole creation.

Talking with God

Sovereign God, forgive us for having too small a vision of who you are, what your eternal plan is, and who you want us to become. Open the eyes of our faith in preparation for the glorious appearance of King Jesus and the glorious consummation of your perfect Kingdom. Give us the humility to learn the greatness of your Kingdom, the beauty of your vision for each of us, and the possibility of moving every earthly organization toward the true prosperity that always marks your Kingdom. We want your Kingdom to come in us and through us and your will to be done in us and through us on earth now as it is in heaven now and as it will someday be in all your creation. Amen.

Questions and Issues

A. What is the practical difference between efficiency and effectiveness? Can you sometimes ignore one or the other? How do you decide which one matters more than the other? Why do followers need to be clear about these two factors? Leaders?

B. What is an important informal or personal role that you have played, or observed someone else play, in addition to a formal organizational role assignment? What difference did it achieve?

C. How does integrity affect the trust of followers under leading with power?

D. Do you generally prefer and/or perform differently as a follower of someone who is leading with power or leading without power? Or is it mostly determined situationally or by some other factor?

E. What situations in any kind of organization can you describe where leadership does not seem to fit one of the four modes as presented here? For example, do these modes fit both healthy and dysfunctional marriages? Dictatorships? Law enforcement? Recovery groups? The UN? Criminal gangs? Bible translation teams? Instagram?

F. Does Jesus Christ lead with power or lead without power or both? What changes, if any, do you expect in his leadership when he fully establishes his Kingdom?

G. Administrative leaders often represent external authority. How might that affect their relationships with followers or the kind of followership they are given by followers?

H. How do the four modes of leading and their corresponding patterns of followership operate in the context of spiritual leadership and the life and fellowship of a local church congregation?

CHAPTER 19

A Model Effectiveness Framework

Effectiveness is achieving a desired condition. It is getting the job done. Tom Jones calls highly effective people *doers* in his book, *Doers: The Vital Few Who Get Things Done.*[25] Whether by doing it all themselves or by organizing followers and their leaders, doers are the people who see what needs to be done, commit to making it happen, avoid all distractions, eliminate barriers, obviate excuses, clarify confusions and contradictions, work collaboratively with mutual respect, and find a way to get it done.

Scott Rodin describes himself as a doer,[26] and his impressive achievements confirm his self-perception, but he challenges leaders (including himself) to understand that your calling is to focus more on becoming who God is calling you to be, and only secondarily on doing what he is calling you to do. The goal is to prioritize *being* over *doing* and repudiate the "doing-first" approach to leadership. Godly doers need organizational support and freedom and a full and clear shared understanding of the desired condition. And they also need a kingdom-centered corporate culture of mutually respectful collaboration and accountability.

Effective leaders work consistently to "create a corporate culture that nurtures followers . . . a corporate culture in which positive change can be sustained because . . . the people who work in these cultures understand how they fit, they feel respected, and they are recognized for their contributions."[27] An effective doer with an inadequate definition of the true desired condition that needs to exist can create collateral damage in the process of achieving that overly narrow vision of success. To be truly effective, every essential element of the desired condition needs to be achieved with-

131

out disrespecting or injuring people or producing any other unacceptable collateral damage in the process. Atchison proposes that effective followers need to choose and support effective leaders with five characteristics:

1. Competence
2. Integrity
3. Consistency
4. Courage
5. Humility[28]

Highly effective doers typically can operate in the follower role or the leader role, and ideally they move fluidly between these roles as needed. Especially if more than one person needs to participate to achieve effectiveness, a comprehensive Effectiveness Framework can help everyone who is involved think together about every human contribution that is needed, who must provide each component, and what risks must be avoided. Such a framework is not itself a detailed project or work plan. Rather, it is a way to ensure that the particular combination of leading and following required for successful development and implementation of such plans are anticipated and provided. Thus, such a framework is also a ready tool for spotting or even anticipating human performance or relational problems and precluding or curing them.

The framework helps to clarify the kinds of following and leading that will be needed and ensure that each role is played by skillful people who have a clear and complete understanding of what they need from others and what others need from them. It could well be called a followership framework because it is mostly as followers that the participants agree on who will provide the necessary leadership and how they, as wise and effective followers, will ensure the leadership effectiveness that is required for success. Done correctly, highly effective individuals form highly effective groups that enjoy the benefits of achieving a vision of wisely chosen desired conditions.

Whether the desired condition involves the whole organization or some defined unit of it, if you get effective following and leading right, you create the best possibility for every person to get the leadership and followership they need for maximum performance in an organization that is successful and good for everyone involved. Ideally, the vision and values of your organization can become ever more aligned with the vision and values of the Kingdom of God, regardless of what kind of organization it is: a family; a taxable or public benefit corporation; a governmental agency or legislative body; a religious organization; a movement. One logical starting point for seeking the Kingdom of God in your organization is for the functions of skillful followership to be exercised in ways that encourage, develop, select, and actively ensure effective leadership. Trying to invert the direction of this process ultimately produces a leader-centric organizational culture whose character and outcomes conflict with those of the Kingdom of God.

The core challenge that followers face in selecting and supporting the necessary leaders is that, despite the accepted core concept that a leader has followers, there clearly are different types of leadership and many types and degrees of followership in diverse contexts. A wise and effective leader is someone whom the necessary people actively and consistently trust and follow to the vision of desired conditions they share.

Because following and leading are mutually defining and interdependent roles, they are two sides of one reality. This concept can be creatively adapted, and can inform the appropriate uses of many other concepts related to leadership and followership, while it also distinguishes what truly is leadership from something else.

The more complex, unpredictable, or threatening a particular vision appears to be, the more important it is to "align expectations so that followers see how they fit into the action plan."[29] An Effectiveness Framework provides a spacious and adaptable way to think and communicate clearly about all the variations of leading and following in any given goal-seeking situation. The framework provided here (see page 135) does not seek to replace or demean any of the alternative ideas, expressions, planning schemes, or project management systems. Rather this framework intends to provide a helpful sample, model, or template with spacious simplicity and dependable consistency in the complexity of organizational reality. It should be referenced and applied with a balance of respect and freedom, discipline and creativity, to help ensure that you have identified all the essential elements that must be provided one way or another for success. Everyone involved needs to be clear about not only who must be effective at what but also who and what they need to enable them to get it done right.

The grid is structured on the four major leadership modes, with a short phrase that describes the main kind of contribution or the importance of that mode of leading in the organization. Displayed under each of the four modes of leadership are twelve elements that are distinctively important for the effectiveness of that particular leadership mode. The word or phrase in each of the fifty-six cells of the table is a short suggestive indicator of a component or aspect of effective organizational following or leading. They can be expanded and adapted to provide a consistent meaning for the dynamic realities of every following-leading situation and relationship across an organization. The resulting conceptual consistency helps improve communication and shared understandings.

The Effectiveness Framework is a tool to help you improve your organizational effectiveness.

1. Identify, clarify, and prioritize the key factors or elements that characterize each of the four major modes of leading related to your situation.

2. Understand and allow for the distinctive effects that each form of leading and following exists to achieve.

3. Envision what followers and leaders need to understand and do to get the right person in the right leadership situation with the necessary support from followers and other leaders to achieve maximum organizational effectiveness.

4. Inform and help evaluate the creation and implementation of processes and plans to achieve the desired condition(s).

Below is an expansion of the summary phrase for each leadership mode in each cell of the model Effectiveness Framework.

A. Lead without power: Lead individuals, teams, a whole organization, or a movement to or toward a compelling future vision through their voluntary followership, without depending on formal organizational authority to require it.

B. Lead with power: Lead followers who are obligated to perform as directed so they can have the benefits of holding a position in a formal structure of organizational authority designed to achieve a desired future condition; or so they can avoid penalties for disobeying an executive order or autocratic threat.

C. Manage: Use defined organizational authority to obtain, organize, and employ the resources and people that achieve objectives that are the measurable elements or indicators of organizational success.

D. Administer: Ensure that all relevant laws and regulations, agency requirements, and organizational policies and principles are properly applied, administered, and satisfied in all activities of the organization.

Effectiveness Framework

Lead without Power	Lead with Power	Manage	Administer
Vision with Influence	Power for Purpose	Objectives with Power	A Code with Authority
A	**B**	**C**	**D**
Personal follower commitment	1. Personal follower commitment	1. Personal follower commitment	1. Personal follower commitment
Voluntary relationship and action	2. Obligatory relationship and action	2. Controlled action	2. Prescribed action
Personal trust-informal	3. Positional power-Formal	3. Positional power-Formal	3. Appropriate behavior-Formal
Personal integrity	4. Corporate integrity	4. Respect for the position	4. Acceptance of the prescription
Improve people and conditions	5. Meet prioritized needs	5. Arrange people and resources	5. Serve people
A healthy organization	6. A successful organization	6. Team Work	6. Bureaucratic dependability
Effectiveness: Do the right thing	7. Power: Do what you want	7. Efficiency: Do things right	7. Orderliness: Do what is permitted
Original art, vision, transformation	8. Strength and capacity	8. Repeatable science	8. Consistent application
Self-expression, creativity	9. Expression of will, action	9. Organizational processes	9. Regulatory control, procedures
Unlimited liability: high risk	10. Risk-reward ratios	10. Limited Liability: low risk	10. Low liability: risk avoidance
Collaboration	11. Confederation	11. Coordination	11. Cooperation
Go to a new future	12. Achieve purposes and goals	12. Achieve objectives	12. Perform properly every time

Meditation

Just as our bodies have many parts and each part has a special function, so it is with Christ's body. We are many parts of one body, and we all belong to each other. In his grace, God has given us different gifts for doing certain things well. . . . Live in harmony with each other. Don't be too proud to enjoy the company of ordinary people. And don't think you know it all. (Romans 12:4-6, 16)

And as long as the king sought guidance from the Lord, God gave him success. . . . But when he became powerful, he also became proud, which led to his downfall. (2 Chronicles 26:5, 16)

The Apostle Paul used the analogy of the human body to recognize the complex challenges of organizing diverse people with different gifts and skills and ideas to follow and lead each other in working for the vision, values, and conditions of the Kingdom of God. Something as basic as loving and serving all other people as you love yourself and serve your own needs is difficult to achieve, and it can even seem self-contradicting. No person knows enough nor is competent enough to succeed all alone. Every situation needs wise and faithful followers to choose and support the right leader. Each person plays a part in a successful harmony of organizational effort that depends on humble learning and sharing by all the participants, followers, and leaders, great and small.

The ancient Hebrew Kings Amaziah and his son Uzziah each served the Lord well as Kings of Judah in Jerusalem during the first part of their reigns. Uzziah even had the benefit of wise counsel from the prophet Zechariah. During their faithful years God prospered their leadership and confirmed that blessing with the strong support of followers who sought to serve the Lord. When leaders sincerely want to please God, they can rightly hope and expect—though not demand—that God will prosper their efforts and bless them with effective support from faithful followership. The critical factor is humility that recognizes God's righteous sovereignty and that acknowledges dependence on the support of wise and faithful followers. However, each of these kings became proud, self-serving, and self-sufficient. They stopped caring about doing what God wanted for the welfare of the followers. So, the followers held their leaders accountable and terminated their leadership.

Talking with God

Heavenly Father, in my following and in my leading, I ask for your Spirit to lead me and all of us into a fuller shared understanding of the complex interactions of all the roles we must fill and the particular functions we each must contribute for us to succeed and grow together. Help each of us see and understand what we must do and why it matters. Help us see how we depend on others and how others depend on us. Make us strong enough and wise enough to achieve our vision together and to be full of your joy with humble and grateful hearts when we get it done. Amen.

Questions and Issues

A. Are some people natural followers or natural leaders? What makes you see them that way?

B. Note: This Framework and this book assume that following and leading are roles that people fill in organizations and relationships, rather than being elements of personal identity. Following is something you do, not who you are. But if you think of yourself as a follower by nature, habit, personality, preference, or giftedness, or if you know someone who does, then consider an excellent book written especially for you by Allen Hamlin Jr., *Embracing Followership*.[30]

C. What are some examples of people whose influence you accept without any apparent active organizational follower engagement with that thought leader? How does that one-way leadership influence happen? By their example or model; their writing; their preaching, teaching, or other public speaking including on the radio, TV, or internet? Do you have any way of exercising the follower functions of informing them or holding them accountable?

D. What are some of your experiences with mutual following and leading at work? At home? In church or other organizational settings?

E. When followers want or need to act together to increase the effectiveness of their influence, do they need leadership among themselves, or can/should it be spontaneous? Is either way better than the other?

F. How do you decide whether a positional leader in your life, at work or in other settings, has the humility, integrity, and competence that makes them safe for you to trust and follow?

G. Have you ever been asked or expected to contribute in some way to something that you felt violated the principles or standards of the Kingdom of God? If so, how did you deal with such a challenge?

Getting the Effective Leadership You Need for Your Best Future

L eadership impacts the whole organization obviously, visibly. But the work of leading is a relatively small proportion of the total work time of most organizations; estimates tend to cluster around 15 percent to 10 percent or less, even when the measurement tries to include every leadership decision or event in every unit or level of the organization every working day. It typically takes much more work time and energy to implement decisions and plans than it does to make them.

How do you get the wise and effective leadership that you need for consistent organizational success? The intuitively simple and obvious part of the answer is that your organization must attract, develop, and retain people who understand the leadership role, are capable of excellence in the role and functions of leading, and are willing to accept the responsibilities and risks in exchange for the rewards you are able to provide.

Almost as obvious as the need for effective leaders throughout the organization is the reality that leadership is also an organizational process that must be constantly nurtured and guided to ensure that everyone understands how the leadership-followership dynamic happens. Every member of a healthy and effective organization understands how they relate to the leadership process and how leadership contributes to their welfare as part of organizational success.

The counterintuitive and not-obvious part of getting the leadership you need is that both the positional and the processive expressions of leadership are products of followership which is—like leadership—an organizational role with various functions. Organizational followers determine who really leads them by deciding whom they are willing—or not willing—to actively follow and support. Kelley put it like this: "If we want high quality leaders, we must seize control of the selection process."[31]

Followers determine the effectiveness of the leadership by how fully and effectively they engage in helping the leader succeed at leading. That followership work includes informing the leader's vision and decisions, affirming and accomplishing the leader's plans, implementing the leader's policies, and encouraging, protecting, defending, and evaluating the leader. The quality, character, and effectiveness of your leadership depends directly on the quality, character, and effectiveness of your followership.

The key to getting wise and effective leadership is wise and effective followership.

Individually and as a group, you make someone your leader and you become their follower to the extent that you accept that person's influence in your thinking, values, beliefs, and/or actions. In formal, hierarchical organizations that influence is grounded in organizational authority or power, but even in that case there is always a voluntary character to followership.

The wisdom and skill of the followers in the process of choosing their leader and making that leader successful determines the quality of leadership in their organization, and that in turn is a decisive factor in the success of the organization. Strong effective leadership is the only true leadership. Weak, ineffective leadership is not leadership, and as so it indicates the absence of effective followership. The strength of a leader is ultimately determined by the total combined strength of the leader's influence and the followers' active engagement and effectiveness. Followership and leadership function interdependently to move the organization toward their shared vision of their desired future conditions, toward how they believe things should be and can be.

Organizational transformation happens in and by the followers.

However, over time, total organizational success depends on the quality of a top to bottom and side to side pervasive culture of effective following and leading. Great organizations do need great leadership, and the more effective that leadership is, the more likely the organization will excel and win and accomplish great Kingdom-ideal results in the world. So, ultimately excellent leadership is created and sustained by excellent followership.

The paradigm of sustainable organizational vitality is followership first. Everyone in a healthy organization is always a follower, and sometimes also a leader. There is no alternative reality.

Effectiveness is achieving the right results, making the desired conditions reality. Achieving effectiveness is getting the right result in the right way, which usually includes doing it as efficiently as possible. Effectiveness is about succeeding, about winning. Effective leadership is essential for organizational health and success, and effective leaders are essential for effective leadership. The only way to get such organizational leadership is to intentionally cultivate and recognize both effective leadership and effective followership. The followership choices and the work of followers determine who leads and how healthy and successful the enterprise will be.

In particular, the top governing body, such as a corporate board of directors, must exemplify the wise followership that chooses leaders who are worthy of their support, and they must show active commitment to all aspects of engaged followership, including holding them accountable. The quality of followership activity in every part of the organization is essential in determining the success of the entire enterprise.

Followers must understand what the work of leadership really is and choose leaders who can do the work of leading excellently. Similarly, the core elements of great followership must be understood, valued, developed, and implemented by everyone throughout the organization.

Leaders require corresponding followers.

An immoral or amoral autocrat cannot rule alone. They must have enough immoral or amoral followers who provide enough power to enforce the autocratic desires, which, in turn, is allowed by enough willing transactional followers who get some specific conditions they desire out of the arrangement. A bad leader needs enough bad followers to stay in power. Similarly, a noble leader must have enough noble followers who share the vision and values of those in leadership roles and actively guide and support those leaders.

Great followership tends to get the leadership they deserve. The same is true of feckless followership.

Effective leaders delegate well. Followership is the primal organizational power especially in the case of a superordinate leader who delegates leadership authority to a subordinate follower. To get the total leadership effectiveness you need for your organization when you delegate formal positional authority, you must commit to do whatever you can to help that delegated leader succeed in moving the organization forward to the agreed desired conditions. That makes you that leader's follower while you also continue as their leader, and similarly, that delegated person is simultaneously your follower and your leader. Each of you must play both roles well to get the necessary leadership effectiveness. It operates in simple dyads and in large populations with complex relationships among multiple leaders and followers.

The core process of a healthy and successful organization is interdependent and skillful following and leading.

Following and leading, and their related skillsets, are universal elements of organizational reality, but they are not innate or genetic. There are no "born leaders or born followers." You learn these basic roles and skills starting during your childhood and youth, and then you refine, enhance, relearn, and prioritize both roles and their related capabilities throughout adulthood as elements of your personality and identity. Most of that adult learning is in organizational settings and systems. So, in a leader-centric culture, leadership development is intentionally valued, studied, developed, and rewarded, while followership learning is typically assumed to just happen somehow.

However, successful people and organizations cannot leave effectiveness in either leading or following to the vagaries of chance and hope things will work out. Because the quality of leadership depends on the quality of followership, intentional training and development of effective followership is just as essential for ongoing organizational health and success as leadership development is. As with leadership, some people seem more adept at following than others, but everyone who is willing to follow well can learn to do it better.

Getting the leadership you need for your organizations starts with developing followership, because your most important act of followership is deciding whom you will follow. As a follower you want a leader who will help you achieve your shared purpose and achieve your desired conditions. Your natural tendency as a follower is to choose and support leaders who:

tell you what you want to hear,

describe what you want to see,

confirm what you want to believe is true,

value, affirm, and praise you for who you are,

protect you from what you fear,

lead you where you want to go,

give you credit for what you do to get there, and

reward your contribution to organizational success.

There is nothing inherently wrong with these natural followership tendencies if they demonstrate wisdom, knowledge, righteous values, and healthy humility. But the Apostle Paul cautioned Timothy about the dangerous people who "will follow their own desires and will look for teachers who will tell them whatever their itching ears want to hear. They will reject the truth and chase after myths" (2 Timothy 4:3-4). This dangerous pattern happens in religious organizations that are by their nature grounded in beliefs that are not subject to empirical evidence, but it also predominates in political organizations and movements—in America and around the world—where natural restraints of fact and logic are replaced by the fears and desires of a special interest bloc and the power of communication media.

Political governmental systems seek to force people to behave certain ways in the hope that their beliefs will come into alignment. Religious systems seek to influence what people believe is true and important so they will behave in accordance with those beliefs. When religious groups—whether Christian, Muslim, Hindu, or any other religion—seek to employ temporal power (legal, electoral, economic, judicial, social, military, organizational, etc.) to force religiously based behavior on nonbelievers, the resulting risk of human hurt and anger is greatly intensified. The seduction of joining religion and politics distorts both elements away from the biblical separation described that is necessary until the Kingdom ideal is achieved under the reign of Christ.

Healthy and effective followers want to hear and see the truth about themselves and the world. And healthy followers who seek first the Kingdom of God want to share in kingdom results that express loving your neighbor as yourself, now in the present earthly realm.

Highly effective followership that seeks first the Kingdom works with leadership to advance love, joy, peace, patience, kindness, goodness, faithfulness, gentleness, and self-control, justice for the weak and poor, redemptive mercy, and the humility to learn how to benefit everyone involved. Great followers want leaders who enhance a shared vision of the best desired future conditions and help them make it happen.

- **Wise and effective followers deserve and tend to be blessed with wise and effective leaders.**

- **Foolish and feckless followers deserve and tend to get leaders like themselves.**

- **Corrupt leaders reward enough corrupt followers to protect their corruption until there is nothing left to take.**

In your role as a follower, you are responsible for participating in the process of choosing and supporting leaders for your organization. You are looking for a person who will be effective at the core functions of the leader role. This process is complicated by the fact that you want a leader who is also a skillful follower. To the extent possible, you want an effective follower who can masterfully fill the leadership role with a servant's heart and who excels at the following core leadership functions.

1. **Clarify the Vision**

   The leader sees farther and more clearly into the future fog than most people, and they seek to provide a true understanding of future realities and their meaning and implications for the organization. They provide prophetic insight that helps you see connections and possibilities from alternative perspectives. They evaluate realities and risks. Ideally, they help you see more clearly the future conditions you *should* want, not just what you might naturally want. And they help you see and value the highest moral, ethical, social, and economic good that can be achieved and the common good of all affected persons, not just your own. They point the way forward to the desired conditions to be achieved in a context that does not yet exist.

2. **Make Decisions**

   An effective leader respects the process of seeking wisdom together, but they require closure and action for change. Effective leadership clarifies, defines, and trusts the decision process, with special attention to who will be consulted and who will actually make the final decision. To get a decision, they may summarize or interpret factors in a way that enables people to agree. They may make subsidiary or contributing decisions that clear the way for agreement on the main issue, including defining the process setting a deadline. When there is no adequate consensus and there are two or more good options, they "break the deadlock" so work can continue. They may delegate a decision to someone else, but they always retain full responsibility, especially if the results are not favorable. Ideally, they make mostly wise decisions that are good for every affected person, but they acknowledge and correct wrong decisions, especially their own, with a different decision. Whoever controls a decision process and/or makes a decision is de facto a functional leader for that organizational event.

3. **Communicate Persuasively**

   A leader is especially effective in the process of presenting, describing, and strengthening commitment for a vision of a desired future condition for the entire organization or for any of its component units. A leader infuses a vision, usually along with the values and conditions that justify that vision, and a sense that it is possible. A leader communicates effectively to build agreements about the vision, policies, strategies, plans, and other decisions needed for taking action. They strengthen group cohesion in support of organizational visions, values, and decisions. They strengthen external support and relationships that advance the success of the organization. Ideally, they convince people with truth and inspire with noble values, including concern for human emotions, not by coercion, threat, or disrespect of any kind. Effective leadership persuasion always demands telling the truth (including about yourself) and doing what is morally and ethically right.

4. **Motivate, Model, and Inspire**

   A leader helps people move from agreement to action. They help people find the courage to let go of the security of the known present condition and move through fear and uncertainty toward the prospect of a different future condition that they hope will eventually be better than what will exist if they try to stay where they are. Ideally, they have credibility to accomplish this motivation by demonstrating willingness to share fully in the challenges and changes involved, including modeling the relevant values and sacrificing their self-interest to advance the common good.

5. **Take Responsibility for Results**

   A leader accurately assesses and explains cause and effect for success and failure. They make necessary changes, especially when failures result from decisions or actions they promoted or approved as a leader. Ideally, they sincerely accept blame for organizational failures, and they acknowledge appropriate followers for successes.

Each core leadership function includes a reference to the ideal. There is morally good leadership and there is morally bad leadership. Whether honorable or evil, leaders have the same foundational leadership functions. Leaders can serve either noble beliefs and values that move organizations and human conditions to be more like the righteous Kingdom of God, or leaders can serve beliefs and values that increase injustice by favoring some people at the expense of others and thus move toward the kingdom of darkness. Unfortunately, as Jean Lipman-Blumen[32] has explained, the "allure of toxic leaders" is a pervasive organizational reality because it is actively supported by the ethical and moral failure of unhealthy followers. Such followers are willing to believe the big lie that they are inherently better and more important than certain other types of humans. Great followers refuse to obey or implement morally flawed directives and will not support toxic leaders who are responsible for such failures.

Communication effectiveness is so important that followers can easily blunder by choosing and elevating leaders for their charisma and communication skills more than their character and leadership competence. Followers sense that they must be convinced to act, and it is common to assume that a convincing communicator is also a visionary leader. However, wise and effective followers choose leaders who listen to them, not just talk to them.

Meditation

> People ruin their lives by their own foolishness and then are angry
> at the Lord. (Proverbs 19:3)

The right leader is someone you can accept responsibility for, someone you can help succeed, someone you can trust with your wholehearted engagement. You make so many of these decisions about leading and following that it is easy to not think and pray about it as you should. And if things do not go as hoped, it is natural to blame the leader whom you chose or blame God whom you did not prayerfully consult, so you can walk away from the whole thing and miss what God wanted to do in you and in everyone else affected by it.

But God is at work when things go badly just as much as when the results are pleasant. God is sovereign over our messes and mistakes just as much as our masterpieces. The result of all the choices by you and everyone else—the wise and the foolish, the gracious and the peevish, the noble and the petty—all work together for good, and ultimately his sovereign plan is achieved in the end of all things. But God offers you the great joy of following him as you choose and follow human leaders to advance the coming of the Kingdom.

Talking with God

Lord, have mercy on our mindless and unjust actions. We need to refuse to follow those who are simply appealing to our flawed set of fears and biases to gain leadership power and its perquisites for themselves by telling us what we want to hear even if it is not true or just.

Lord, have mercy on us in our self-deception. False leaders confirm our desire to believe that we are wise when what we believe is actually delusional folly. Selfish leaders will convince us to follow their example of serving ourselves and ignoring the needs of others. Narcissistic leaders will trick us into thinking that their vengeful self-advancement is morally right for us to approve and emulate.

Lord, have mercy when as followers we must decide who will lead us. Shine your light into the darkness of our deceitful hearts and show us the people who should take on the work of leading. In matters great and small teach us to choose our leaders wisely and support them well, so that there is no blaming or shaming because we lead and follow together for the greatness of your Kingdom. Amen.

Questions and Issues

A. How can followers understand who would and would not be the leaders that deserve their support? What do they need in order to choose well? How do you develop and maintain the necessary wise and effective followership?

B. Have you or someone you know ever decided to leave a job or an organization because of leadership issues? If so, what was the core problem?

C. If organizational transformation must ultimately happen in and by the followers, what is the meaning, importance, or function of "transformational leadership"?

D. What are the keys to effective interdependence of leading and following? Have you seen or been part of a relationship with simultaneous leading and following by both parties? If so, what were the results?

E.   What are the negative results of a leader who cannot follow well? Can you describe an effective board member or other high-level leader who demonstrates effectiveness in both servant-followership and servant-leadership?

F.   What can prevent bad followers from supporting bad leaders to get unjust benefits for themselves? In for-profit companies? Nonprofits? Government? Church?

G.   What can be done to create safety and encouragement for followers to contribute information that leaders might not welcome or that might need further investigation, especially if it relates to accountability concerns?

H.   What other core leadership functions might not be adequately identified in the five functions listed here?

I.   What important lessons have you learned from being part of search processes to fill leadership positions? What leads to excellent results? What leads ultimately to failed leadership?

J.   How could the Effectiveness Framework help ensure a successful employment search process, performance evaluation process, or program review? What could make the framework useless or even counterproductive?

K.   How can followers discern who will and won't listen well and also be decisive?

L.   What potentially critical elements of character, competence, or commitment might be missing from the lists provided?

Getting the Effective Followership You Need from Your Phantasmagoria

U ltimately the quality and effectiveness of organizational leadership depends on the character, competence, commitment, and overall effectiveness of its followership. Effective followership approves, supports, and empowers effective leadership. Fully engaged followership does the work that achieves the desired conditions that leadership describes and promotes. Effective followership gets the job done for organizational health and success. Weakness in any area of followership will show in the effectiveness of leadership. Getting the organizational success you want depends on the collaboration of great leadership and great followership, and the followership.

Organizational leading and following can both be developed and strengthened precisely because neither one is an identity. Identity has to do with who you are. Your identity is mostly comprised of fundamental elements of your personhood. A role and its functions are something you learn to do.

An effective leader is a person who has the support of effective followers who have chosen their leader by accepting that leader's influence to some degree in some part of their life. That reality makes leading and following interdependent and mutually defining elements of organizational reality and activity. Leading and following are the two comprehensive organizational roles, but these two sides of the organizational coin have one enormous difference.

The role, function, and importance of leadership make that role empirically visible. You see leadership in position titles, job descriptions, organizational charts. You see it in research reports, book titles, course descriptions, websites, and seminars. You see it any time someone initiates change or makes a decision that people support. In countless contexts from politics to religion, you can see who is in charge. Leadership feels real and important.

In stark contrast, the role, functions, and importance of followership are not empirically observable like leadership. Followership does not seem to exist in the way that leadership exists. What does effective following look like? What is following supposed to accomplish? How do you evaluate and develop and strengthen something so broad, variable, vague, and changeable? You can evaluate leadership success and make changes as needed, but evaluating and trying to improve the followership that gets it all done is a lot fuzzier.

Leadership is stable and dependable, with an all-or-nothing quality and with evident responsibilities for certain decisions and the results. There is no sort-of or half-way leadership. Either you are the leader at any point, or you are not. Either you are in or out. The leader is openly responsible for organizational success and failure. These characteristics of leadership largely explain the dominant leader-centric model with its strong focus on leadership development. That professional development priority on leadership silently or implicitly acknowledges that followers make leaders. So, leadership development literature and training often include enhancing the leader's ability to attract, hold, and strengthen the followership by which their leadership is defined, supported, and evaluated.

You have a leader partly so that you have someone to blame if the effort fails. This is not a humorous aphorism. It is a statement of fact. You cannot fire the whole team, or disband the political party, or release all the professors, or dismiss all the medical staff, or disenfranchise all the voters. Very rarely will all the followers agree to blame themselves for an organizational failure. Instead, you get a new leader.

The daunting problem with developing high-quality followership—which is not the same thing as hiring competent employees or recruiting skill volunteers—is that followership is inherently invisible, unstable, and unpredictable, with limited and contingent commitments, a partial or mixed role identity, and unresolvable paradoxes.

Followership operates on a continuum from sort-of, slightly, and sometimes supporting a certain leader in a certain situation, to being totally committed and willing to sacrifice and even die for the leader and their shared vision and values. A follower may not even admit to being a certain leader's follower, supporter, or defender, while actually practicing multiple dimensions of strong followership for that leader. And the exact reverse of that case is also common: publicly praising the leader while doing nothing to advance the leader's success.

Compared with the stable character of leadership, followership is a shadowy, shifting, and disorderly phantasmagoria of fleeting figments that seem to defy systemized efforts to define and measure its existence, strength, or effectiveness, let alone attempt to develop and enhance it. To make it worse, positional leaders often control decisions about who gets what kind of professional development, and many leaders instinctively fear a possible threat to their power and prerogatives if followership is stronger, more self-aware, more fully informed, and more capable of holding them accountable.

In a formal organization it is typically clear who reports to whom in the hierarchy and thus it is clear who is an obligatory follower and who their formal positional leaders are. The leadership authority exists even if not one person voluntarily wants to follow and support that position or the leader who holds that title. If you want to keep your job, you are obligated to perform as required by the "leadership." Such obligatory followers are clearly identified. But, even with opinion polls and focus groups, it is not overtly clear how committed any given individual or group of followers actually is to their leader at any moment on any leadership factor or issue.

The amorphous force of voluntary followership is a constantly changing field of perceptions, feelings, beliefs, values, commitments, images, assumptions, memories, hopes, and fears that can vary by the day, the moment, the issue, an expression, a baseless rumor, or a prophesy—true or false. Followership can range from irresistible to barely perceptible, and from unrestrained passionate commitment to the weakest possible level of begrudging minimal compliance. You can decide to be a committed follower or a follower in name only and nobody needs to know.

The basis of deep or primal followership can be personal relationship, belief, vision, value, fear, hope, financial benefits, or any of a score of other factors. Followership can even be grounded in a complete fantasy, a myth, belief, prejudice, or image that has no basis in fact, and followership can give enormous power to a person who is not a credible or honorable leader by any real-world definition. Variations of the word "lead" and the title "leader" occur often in job descriptions. "Follow" occurs in expressions like "follow instructions," but "follower" is not a title or term used in job descriptions and evaluations, though the tasks and desired results of following are often carefully named and evaluated. And with a notable twist of irony, you can talk about servant-leaders but rarely is there any reference to servant-followers. Formal organizations refer to subordinates, but that is a different concept from followers.

The followers on one side of the organizational coin determine whose face they are willing to have on the other side.

There are degrees of effectiveness in a leadership role or position, but there are no degrees of leadership. Leadership can be formal or informal, momentary or long enduring. There are many modes, kinds, styles, and contextual versions of leading, but either a particular person in a particular situation is a leader or not. This overtly empirical characteristic of leading makes leadership analysis and development logical and achievable. That reality contrasts sharply with the covert, variegated, partial-hearted, and qualified nature of the following that creates and sustains that leadership. There is no simple, objective, consistent way to be certain whether a person or a group of persons is or is not a leader-making follower or how strong and durable that followership is. There are no degrees of the leadership role, but there certainly are degrees of followership.

The response to this fundamental difference of identity and role has been to focus on developing the leaders you need and hope that they can attract and influence the followership the leaders need. Leadership is considered more important than following, and serving as a leader is more valued and has more status and rewards than serving as a follower. Leadership is considered worth studying and developing, and followership is not considered to be worth studying or intentionally trying to develop. But the fact remains that ultimately followers decide who the leaders are and how successful their leadership is. The leader-centric model is not consistently improving the socio-economic values and conditions that serve the common good. On every continent and in every category of organizations the gaps in well-being, justice, opportunity, and hope between the rich and powerful and the poor and powerless are severe and widening.

So, in the absence of a followership development effort corresponding to the leadership development focus, and, given that any single follower has less organizational power than a leader, followers often form an organization of some kind in an effort to match leadership power with followership power. The tyranny of the followers responding to the tyranny of leaders is obvious in contexts like electoral politics and labor unions, but it is increasingly significant in many other settings as followers recognize their unified power potential. The voluntary followership in such situations can fall to the lowest level of minimal obedience, doing only and exactly what the positional leader commands, even if it is foolish. Good faith collaboration of leading and following is replaced with various kinds of power-based conflict that is waged from board rooms and court rooms to the polarized media and violence in the streets. There is a better way.

Following and leading are equally important complementary roles.

The better way begins with the desire to build a better model that seeks to advance the values and human conditions of the Kingdom of God in all types of organizations and in their effects on people and the world in which they live. The better way recognizes that leading and following are equally important roles that every organizational member must understand and be able to fill as needed for the organization to succeed. The better way intentionally develops effective followership in every position for engagement in every decision, process, and system. The better way develops effective followership that chooses its leadership wisely, supports its leadership with full commitment and skillful engagement, and holds its leadership accountable for achieving effectiveness with ethical and moral excellence.

Followership development begins with seeing, understanding, and valuing followership as a role in which everyone in the organization must be reasonably competent. Followership development seeks to improve performance in all the core functions and contributions for which the follower role is responsible. The effectiveness of the followership development effort must be evaluated in relation to the distinctive culture of the organization and the functional effectiveness of its leadership.

Thus, the followership core functions support, implement, balance, and constrain the core functions of leadership depending on what is needed and what leadership welcomes or resists. The core functions of leadership or followership operate in relationship to their counterparts. Competence in executing each of the core followership functions needs to be systematically taught, learned, and celebrated. And followership competencies must be intentionally referenced, developed, respected, evaluated, and rewarded. Each member of the organization should be able to sense at all times whether they need to be contributing as a follower or as a leader and move fluidly between the two roles as the situation requires. These are not identities. They are learned roles and skills of following.

1. **Verify a Vision**

    The default starting point of effective followership on any visionary description, prediction, proposal, or plan is respectful doubt and responsible skepticism. The farther into the obscuring future fog the vision stretches, or the more a vision of the present reality contradicts currently controlling presumptions, the stronger the followers' instinctive reticence must be expressed. The past and the present can be described and understood with facts from objective analysis and subjective experience. But the future can only be projected on assumptions, hopes, beliefs, or guestimates. Followers rightly need to be confident that the future desired conditions are worth the risks of leaving what is known and losing what is good from their current experiential reality. The greater and faster the change appears to be, the more intensely followers question, test, and require compelling facts and logic. Followership is grounded in the consensus about current reality, and the worse the present reality is, the more justifiable major change becomes.

    In cases where the followership consensus cannot confidently verify the future vision or plan directly, effective followers must verify based on their informed trust in the leader whom they helped choose. Normally, the followership responsibility is to consider the vision or plan, help modify it as needed, and either reject it and refuse to help make it happen, or else verify it as true and worthy by working to realize the vision or implement the plan.

2. **Identify and Inform Decisions That Need to Be Made**

Effective followership is responsible for seeing what is wrong in a current situation or in a vision or plan. Effective followership says or does something about any such problematic situation. Feckless followership accepts no such responsibility to seek a decision for change, unless the situation appears to directly threaten their self-interest. The problem may be barely perceptible or just slightly less than optimal, or it could be a major issue that is physically, financially, or morally dangerous. If there is a change that an effective follower can appropriately implement, they will do so, but either way they report it and persist until leadership is aware and fully informed and makes a decision about it. To the extent possible, the effective follower finds ways to identify problems and raise concerned awareness with a positive and irenic and gracious spirit that leads to consensual action for positive change for the organization. But it must be done one way or another.

3. **Hold Leaders (and Followers) Accountable**

Because followers—individually or en masse—determine whom they accept to lead them, effective followership must hold that leadership accountable. However, holding leadership accountable can be risky business. Doing so may make followers endure resistance, criticism, ostracization, or other punitive actions including losing their job, so followership development must include encouragement and protection of this vital activity. Otherwise, the followership accountability function dissipates instead of being robust and respected.

Any one person functioning in the follower role is inherently less powerful and more vulnerable than they are in a leadership role. They can often feel personally or professionally threatened for raising a problem or reporting a concern, especially one involving a powerful leader or a popular program or principle. To help ensure healthy followership, a healthy organization allows or even encourages followers to speak and act together for important principles, and it provides an absolutely safe system to protect an individual "whistleblower" and encourages them to report what they think needs, or appears to need, investigation or action. The follower role is not responsible for solving such problems or addressing needs that might deserve or require organizational attention, but followers are responsible for leadership accountability, and also for holding each other accountable in the shared work of implementing the approved plans and standards.

4. **Support and Implement (Only) Pragmatic Promises and Plans**

    Effective followership relies on leadership for decisions about direction, so it includes a mindset of willingness to be persuaded and to support worthy ideas. But effective followership refuses to willingly attempt to implement any leadership proposal that they know or believe from their experience is likely or certain to fail. Leadership must understand and reference trends, fact-based theories, and guiding principles of good practice that may not yet be generally known. Followership must consistently and appropriately apply the test of real-world facts and experience in evaluating leadership promises, proposals, and plans, but effective followership also must provide the support, expertise, and energy that implement approved plans and make progress possible. Informed followership is essential for implementing plans and promises that pass the pragmatism test. Constant purposeful change marks the culture of successful organizations, and effective followership cultivates a culture of readiness to follow and support wise leadership for progress. But blind or silent followership deprives leadership of a unique source of practical wisdom, and that lacuna can produce catastrophic results for your organization.

5. **Provide Momentum**

    Organizational momentum comes from followership not leadership. Effective communication by leadership can convince people that something is true, relevant, important, needs to be done, and can be achieved. Effective leadership can inspire with a stirring call to the organizational action that is needed to avoid the dire consequences of remaining who you are and staying where you are. The leader may metaphorically, or actually, scream and run toward the new condition. But until the followers move, there is stasis. Without momentum nothing changes.

Momentum is the product of the mass and the speed of a moving body. The faster and harder and larger the mass of followership moves toward the goal, the more likely the organizational momentum will be adequate to overcome resistance of every kind and reach the desired condition. Leaders cannot carry the weight or create the total energy of the mass of moving followership. Instead, leaders ride the wave of organizational momentum produced by effective followers.

These primary functions of the follower role operate in dynamic tension with the counterpart functions of the leadership role. The reality of that tension by itself presents a worthy challenge to evaluating, developing, and consistently achieving effective following. However, most of the time the challenge is further intensified by several unresolvable paradoxes, except for the situations when a follower is also simultaneously playing the leadership role. The potentially paradoxical expectations of effective following include these examples adapted from a longer compilation developed by Gene Dixon.[33]

Paradoxes of an effective follower:

- has their own vision versus attracted to the leader's vision,

- remains fully responsible for their own actions versus concedes considerable authority to the leader,

- responsible for implementing the leader's ideas versus responsible for challenging and improving the leader's ideas, and

- is a group member versus challenges group-think

There is more than this to effective followership in any situation, but not usually less. The intentional development of effective following in your organization begins with enhancing awareness and performance of these core functions and paradoxical challenges of the followership role. The strategies and methods used may be similar to those you use for leadership training and development. But there are four significant differences between leadership development and followership development.

First. Almost everyone in your organization understands and accepts the importance of leadership. They might not be able to give you a good working definition of what it is, but they know from experience that it matters, and they can accept the premise that it is important to improve leadership effectiveness. But typically, almost no one in your organization recognizes the importance of improving effectiveness in the followership role. Indeed, the first reaction of many would be a negative assumption that the purpose of such an effort would be to simply strengthen compliant obedience to leadership directives.

Second. Leadership training is a well-developed industry with countless consultants, books, articles, seminars, videos, workbooks, and discussion guides, but with followership development, not so much, though materials and consulting are available.

Third. Leadership development is usually selective; it is provided to a relatively small proportion of people with recognized organizational leadership roles. Those favored few who are chosen to receive leadership development are people who appear to need it, and/or who deserve it, and/or who seem capable of benefiting from it for the good of the organization. Organizations need many more followers than leaders at any given moment, but role training is disproportionately invested in the leadership minority, rather than in improving the followership ability of everyone in the whole organization.

There is significant evidence that "for all the time, enormous human resources, and money spent on promoting leadership and learning, our ROI has been low."[34] If leadership development were the primary cause of organizational excellence, then, around the world, the indicators of a healthy society that serves the common good should be improving rather than worsening. The world certainly needs better strategies that provide better organizational leadership, including political leadership, from the small minority of the world population that holds such positions. But typically, there are no position descriptions that identify certain followers who deserve special followership development, and the working assumption is that the rest do not need it. The reality is that everyone, and especially those in formal leadership positions, can benefit from enhancing their followership insights and effectiveness.

Fourth. Like leadership, there are many kinds or types of followership. Followership can be positional and/or situational, and there are different styles of followership. But unlike leadership, there are degrees of every kind or type of followership, as each follower or group of followers determines the extent or intensity of their followership of any particular leadership influence. Organizational followership development must consistently and creatively allow for the constantly changing reality of the shifting components, contradictions, and degrees of intensity of the followership phantasmagoria.

With these four differences in mind, you can design and launch an ongoing commitment to followership development. The broad and deep benefits of improving followership effectiveness demonstrate that operationalizing the values of the Kingdom with attention to servant followership is "good business" in the long run. And failure to invest in developing more effective followership in pursuit of kingdom values invites organizational imbalance, injustice, and dysfunction that drags organizations, systems, societies, and nations downward.

Including everyone in efforts to enhance followership effectiveness does present a very different kind of challenge than the pattern of selecting a few people for leadership development. However, there are four basic guidelines that can help you initiate or enhance a culture of followership development in your organization.

1. Start followership training at "the top and the bottom" more or less simultaneously with the board and C-suite members of formal leadership and the lowest paid tier of employees and/or volunteers.

2. Depend primarily on the participants to teach, learn, and encourage each other in their training groups, with some basic learning materials, a schedule or structure to frame the process, and a person or small group authorized to help make the process successful with some flexible financial support.

3. Start or improve information flow in all directions with transparency that includes strategies like a dedicated website, open-book management, and sharing key performance indicator data internally to make relevant ideas, information, and learning activities available to all members of the organization.

4. Ensure that everyone understands and can explain how their work relates to the success of others and of the success of the organization as a whole.

The broad and deep benefits of improving followership effectiveness demonstrate that operationalizing the values of Kingdom stewardship with attention to servant followership is "good business" in the long run. Failure to invest in developing more effective followership in pursuit of kingdom values invites organizational imbalance, injustice, and dysfunction that drags organizations, systems, societies, and nations downward.

The comprehensive inclusion of everyone in efforts to enhance followership effectiveness presents a very different kind of challenge than the pattern of selecting a few people for leadership development. However, there are four basic guidelines that can help you initiate or enhance a culture of followership development in your organization.

1. Provide followership training at "the top and the bottom" more or less simultaneously with the board and C-suite members of formal leadership and the lowest paid tier of employees and/or volunteers.

2. Depend primarily on the participants to teach, learn, and encourage each other in their training groups, with some basic learning materials, a schedule or structure to frame the process, and a person or small group authorized to help make the process successful with some flexible financial support.

3. Ensure information flow in all directions with strategies like a dedicated website, open-book management, and sharing key performance indicators to make relevant ideas, activities, and organizational data available to all members of the organization.

4. Ensure that everyone understands and can explain how their work relates to the success of others and of the organization as a whole.

For redeemed followers of Jesus Christ, the main thing is to always seek first the Kingdom of God. The Kingdom is the organizational model or ideal where everything is done by effective servant-followers who wisely choose and support certain fellow-followers to be their servant-leaders, so that each person and the organization as a whole demonstrate effective stewardship of kingdom resources under the sovereignty of God for the glory of Christ the King.

The main thing is the King and his Kingdom.

Meditation

Before the Passover celebration, Jesus knew that his hour had come to leave this world and returned to his Father. He had loved his disciples during his ministry on earth, and now he loved them to the very end. It was time for supper, and the devil had already prompted Judas, son of Simon Iscariot, to betray Jesus. Jesus knew that the Father had given him authority over everything and that he had come from God and would return to God. So, he got up from the table, took off his robe, wrapped a towel around his waist, and poured water into a basin. Then he began to wash the disciples' feet, drying them with the towel he had around him.

When Jesus came to Simon Peter, Peter said to him, "Lord, are you going to wash my feet?"

Jesus replied, "You don't understand now what I am doing, but someday you will."

"No," Peter protested, "you will never ever wash my feet!"

Jesus replied, "Unless I wash you, you won't belong to me."

Simon Peter exclaimed, "Then wash my hands and my head as well, Lord, not just my feet!"

Jesus replied, "A person who has bathed all over does not need to wash, except for the feet, to be entirely clean. And you disciples are clean, but not all of you." For Jesus knew who would betray him. That is what he meant when he said, "Not all of you are clean."

After washing their feet, he put on his robe again and sat down and asked, "Do you understand what I was doing? You call me 'Teacher' and 'Lord' and you are right, because that's what I am. And since I, your Lord and Teacher, have washed your feet, you ought to wash each other's feet. I have given you an example to follow. Do as I have done to you. I tell you the truth, slaves are not greater than their master. Nor is the messenger more important than the one who sends the message. Now that you know these things, God will bless you for doing them." (John 13:1-17)

It is ironic that most organizations can justify resources to help a relatively small percentage of their members learn how to lead better when a situation calls for leadership actions, but they do not justify helping everyone in the organization learn how to follow well, which they all need to do well, all the time. This tendency is doubly ironic given the reality that as followers you ultimately determine who your leaders are, and you believe that effective leadership is essential for success.

Jesus lived his personal example of humbly serving his followers. He also gave his clear instruction for his followers to serve each other in the same way that he came to serve, not to be served. If you accept his example and his teaching, then logically you also understand that the King has explained the foundational character of servant-followership for all organizational titles, positions, and roles as you implement his instruction to make his Kingdom your top priority in everything you do. Jesus did not call people to enroll in his leadership training program so they would know how to be in charge after he departed. He invited them to follow him and serve others. They promised to follow him even to death. A few hours later they had all abandoned him.

The heavenly realm of the Kingdom of God is a perfectly ordered organization of servant-followers supporting servant-leaders in collaborative stewardship of all creation under God's sovereign authority. When Christ the King returns to earth, he will rule over one unified Kingdom of Heaven and earth. He will make all things right, including a perfectly ordered organization of organizations where servant-followers and servant-leaders collaborate to the glory of their King. Neither role will be more or less important. That Kingdom is our organizational ideal now. But it is easy to be so attracted by powerful leadership that we ignore the equally important role and power of followership in practicing stewardship of the Kingdom of God under the authority of Christ the King.

Every organization on earth is ultimately under God's sovereign rule whether they acknowledge it or not. And even those persons who own an organization under human laws are responsible with all the other members of the organization to act as stewards, not as greedy and selfish managers while the King is physically away.

God offers every person the privilege of choosing to follow Jesus Christ, the one true and ultimate King. God also offers every person the privilege of learning to serve first and always as a follower. In that follower role you wisely choose and supportively follow and support human leaders, and you accept the servant-leadership role when wise followers call you to do so. In the leader role you are to lead with a heart and mind of servant-followership. God offers every person the privilege of seeking to become more like Christ the King and working to move every organization toward the ideal of his coming Kingdom.

Talking with God

> *Living God, consuming fire, purge the self-centered sin from our lives. By your Spirit of power and Word of truth fill our hearts with a singular desire to understand how to seek first your Kingdom in all we do, from family to church and every other organization we are part of. Lord, have mercy and warn us when we seek first to be served, instead of to serve, and when we seek first to be in charge and assert our will, instead of seeking first to learn servant-followership and doing your will. Teach us to wash each other's feet as we seek your Kingdom in your way. For Jesus' sake, amen.*

Questions and Issues

A. Given that leader-centrism is the predominant cultural norm from job titles to book and course titles, what are some ways that the broader and more inclusive reality of followership can be recognized and integrated along with its leadership counterpart? In job descriptions? Performance evaluations? Awards (for exceptionally effective, creative, or courageous followership, etc.)? A type of diversity or perspective required on committees or other work teams, that is, to not just include a "staff representative" but an "effective follower"? Course titles and syllabi? What else?

B. Could your organizations provide professional development programs for people who want—or need—to strengthen their followership effectiveness? Or include everyone, starting at the top of the hierarchy, to set an example and because it is most significant and valuable there, and too often missing or invisible?

C. Some organizations have "listening groups." Could these and other similar processes explicitly recognize, describe, and encourage the role and functions of active followership?

D. How might organizational language be updated and enhanced with explicit references to followership? For examples: servant-leaders serve followers; followers help inform and evaluate their leaders; followers and their leaders are working to resolve this problem.

E. What would some key benefits be of equalizing the status of followership and leadership in an organization? What new challenges or problems might it create?

F. What questions or doubts do you have about any aspect of any of the followership functions offered here to describe the work of following?

G. To what extent does the explanation of followership in momentum agree or disagree with your understanding of this phenomenon in organized groups or social movements? How does this operate with media "followers" on the internet?

H. What potentially important functions of the followership role might be missing from the descriptions provided here?

I. How real are the paradoxes of an effective follower as shown here? In practice, how relevant or problematic are such paradoxes? Are such paradoxes unique to followership, or does leadership have its own set?

J. In organizational life, what are examples of leaders washing the dusty feet of their followers as Jesus did?

CHAPTER 22

Countless Categories of Fractional Followership

A mong his followers there was no doubt that Jesus was always the leader, but like any group, the support of any single follower focused on different factors, and trust could vary from moment to moment and from issue to issue. Each follower liked certain things Jesus did or said, and each wanted to see, hear, or encourage more such things. They also doubted, questioned, and even chastened him. Many followed enthusiastically for a while and then dropped out completely when Jesus did not lead in directions they approved.

Jesus invited many individuals to follow him and thus make a more complete and enduring commitment to him as their leader. He asked them to make a strong and explicit promise to actively learn, understand, and accept what he was teaching, and to actively support and work for the kingdom he described and for him as its leader.

Some of those whom Jesus personally invited refused his invitation. Twelve of those who did accept his offer formed an inner circle of his closest and most committed followers. But the understanding, motivations, acceptance, support, commitment, and faithfulness even among those twelve disciples varied greatly over time and under changing circumstances. At one time or another, each of the twelve doubted him. Eventually, all twelve fell far short of full faith and acceptance and one of them actively betrayed him.

A follower has a leader whose influence they accept to some degree relative to one or more of the follower's values or desired conditions. Even for the unique case of choosing to follow Jesus, the one perfect leader, learning to fully follow Jesus is a life-long process of ups and downs; following is a partial and time-limited commitment. So, even within the bounded context of a single organization, most people follow multiple leaders in various ways and with varying degrees of trust and engagement on matters that vary from huge to tiny and from decades to a few moments.

The exceptions to this pattern of following multiple leaders are rare and tend to be unhealthy, such as a cultic pattern in which the followers believe whatever their leader says is true, regardless of any contradicting evidence, and they do whatever the leader tells them to do, even if it is bad or deadly for them. Except for such extreme cases, most people have many sources of leadership influence that they trust to varying degrees for varying reasons and in diverse parts of their organizational and personal lives.

Follower Case: Following Is My Job

This job I have right now—I can't afford to lose it. So, no matter what they tell me to do, I do my best to comply without questioning, look supportive, and try to succeed and avoid trouble. Even when I think I have a better idea, I don't say anything because I am not one of the "chosen few" that management listens to. The head of my department is a decent person, but he seems threatened by my college degree, and sometimes he seems uncertain about how to relate to me because I'm a woman. So, I have to be careful to protect myself from his insecurity. I agree with him and encourage him as much as I can, and I don't question or even raise alternatives to his proposals or decisions. He's my boss and my job is to help him succeed at what he decides for us to do.

I feel that if I would get evaluated for creativity or taking initiative, I would not get as strong a rating as I think I am capable of, but that's better than losing my job. I justify giving him positive evaluations on the annual performance assessments by comparing him to a bad leader rather than a great one. They tell us the evaluations are anonymous, but some of us aren't sure about that, so I do not risk it. If I were asked directly if I support him, I would say yes. And I think that would be a reasonably true response. I'm getting paid to accomplish what he assigns, not to keep him from making mistakes or looking bad. His job is leading us. My job is following and supporting him.

In sharp contrast with the all-or-nothing character of leading, following is fractional. There are countless varieties and variations of followership, and each is a fraction of some mythical maximum from 99 percent to zero.

In your follower role, you reserve the right to decide how much authority or weight you give to any one source of influence on your thinking and behavior related to any specific situation. It's not simplistic; it's complicated, but in very different ways from the complications of leadership. There are many kinds of leadership and many leadership styles and countless situations. There also are countless kinds and categories of followership, but, unlike leadership, followership is inherently fractional, partial, conditional, and changeable. So, there are degrees of every type of followership, from minimum to maximum and from momentary to life long.

One major source of followership complication is the growing proportion of impersonal or mediated leadership influence from someone the follower does not personally know. For example, you might trust your pastor whom you know personally for insights and guidance about biblical concepts of salvation or social justice ministry. But for the best way to reconcile the Genesis account of God's creation of humans with the prevailing scientific data, you might give more credence to the concepts you found in a book and video by a Christian scholar at a Christian university. In that case, you trust and follow a remote thought leader whom you have never personally met more than you trust a person you know.

"Influencers" on TV or the internet have "followers." So, by definition, that makes them leaders, though often such media influencers do not lead any formal or informal organization and the followers typically are not connected with each other. Followership "support" in such cases is typically impersonal—the followers send money, provide marketing or public opinion data, and so forth. This kind of media-based leading and following is increasingly common, especially in religious, social, or political movements. Social media and 24-hour information channels create interest clusters and thought leaders using algorithms that increase the amount and visibility and narrow the focus of content that is offered to any given individual. Viewers and readers, viewed as followers, respond more often and more strongly to polarizing negative or fear-based images and messages than to positive ones. This kind of following is fractional and insular, and it changes as the importance of an issue or problem rises and falls.

Followership in organizations involves ongoing personal decisions about how any organizational element relates to factors like a follower's employment status, personal values, or the vision of the shared purpose that holds followers and their leaders together. The bond between followers and leaders is grounded in their shared purpose, the future condition that followers and their leaders desire for themselves and for their organization. Thus, the nature, intensity, power, engagement, courage, visibility, and effectiveness of followership are all variable over time. That reality makes followership more difficult to see, assess, and categorize than leadership. But more significantly, it makes improving followership wisdom and effectiveness more difficult than improving leadership.

As Ira Chaleff convincingly explains, the power imbalance between leaders and their followers means that courage is an essential requirement for the highest kinds of effective followership.[35] Courage is also often needed for effective leadership, but courageous followers typically face greater risks with less protection than leaders have. Courage is the opposite of cowardice. Cowardice is failure to fulfil your duty because of fear. It is a character flaw, but in everyday life, with exceptions like the military and first responders, cowardice has become so common that it is usually euphemistically called other things—such as prudence or self-care—and thus cowardice is routinely ignored, excused, or justified. Courage, by contrast, is more rare and thus more noticeable and more honored, with a few common exceptions such as command-and-control power leaders who do not appreciate having courageous followers that question them, speak truth to them, or hold them accountable.

Recognizing and praising the courage of great followership is an important element in followership development. Though usually formed in childhood, courage comes from a person's inner character that can be continuously developed and strengthened throughout life. Courageous followership is urgently needed in a leader-centric environment. The first step in enhancing followership effectiveness is to enable followers to recognize and value their own followership. Even highly effective followership is inherently fractional and variable over time and changing situations, not singular, holistic, fixed, or permanent. The types and degrees of engagement and intensity on each continuum prevent any kind standard scale, taxonomy or matrix. The terms you use to assess and develop effective followership might include some of the following examples and their opposites: trust, integrity, competence, courage, commitment, wisdom, caring, determination, dedication, values, honesty, engagement, credibility.

Leaders naturally tend to prefer Implementers who affirm the leader's vision and work effectively to make it happen. But the followers who effectively challenge the leader when challenge is needed are equally essential in the long run. There are other typologies; each one can be helpful in one situation or another. You have the privilege of gaining insights from all of them as you devise the most useful way to describe and enhance the followership that your organization needs for each of the four main kinds of leadership in the Effectiveness Framework.

Effective following is a complicated and constantly changing reality, but understanding and developing it sure beats the alternative of simplistic leader-centrism in shaping earthly organizations to become more like kingdom organizations.

Meditation

> So they arrested him and led him to the high priest's home. And Peter followed at a distance. The guards lit a fire in the middle of the courtyard and sat around it, and Peter joined them there. A servant girl noticed him in the firelight and began staring at him. Finally she said, "This man was one of Jesus' followers!"
>
> But Peter denied it. "Woman," he said, "I don't even know him!"
>
> After a while someone else looked at him and said, "You must be one of them!"
>
> "No, man, I'm not!" Peter retorted.
>
> About an hour later someone else insisted, "This must be one of them, because he is a Galilean, too."
>
> But Peter said, "Man, I don't know what you are talking about." And immediately, while he was still speaking, the rooster crowed.
>
> At that moment the Lord turned and looked at Peter. Then Peter remembered that the Lord had said, before the rooster crows tomorrow morning, you will deny three times that you even know me." And Peter left the courtyard, weeping bitterly. (Luke 22:54-62)

A personal decision to follow Jesus and put his Kingdom above all other priorities should be the one great exception to the incessant vagaries of the roles and functions and degrees of commitment, intensity, and energy in all the subsidiary elements of following and leading. That decision to follow Jesus Christ does change who you are. It gives you a new identity and a permanent unmitigated commitment as a servant-follower, servant-leader, and steward of resources in his Kingdom. From then on everything you do in every relationship and organization is kingdom-first, no matter what style of followership or which kind of leadership is needed for wise decisions and effective action in all the situations that you meet.

But even that most profound life-defining relationship with Jesus Christ is subject to change, despite having a perfect leader, as Judas and Peter and the rest of the twelve disciples demonstrated. So, it is understandable that in all our other events and relationships of following other fallen humans who are just as fallible as we are, under constantly changing conditions, our following is fractional and flexible for each situation. Learning to constantly improve all that following is an ongoing pursuit for each person individually and also for the organizational process of helping each other see, understand, and enhance following.

Talking with God

Heavenly Father, we want our actions to agree with our prayer for your kingdom to come soon and for your will to be done in our lives and in the affairs of all our organizations. As followers of Jesus, we want all our following among our imperfect fellow humans to be wise and effective as we wait with great anticipation for our King Jesus Christ to come with power and glory to establish his Kingdom of the New Heaven and the New Earth. We long for our organizations now to be as much like that great Kingdom as possible.

As followers we must decide who leads us, and our followership is a constantly changing scene made up of many elements. That reality makes our followership development difficult to conceptualize, evaluate, and improve. But difficult is not impossible. Given what is at stake from the leader-centric model that presently dominates, and the increasing amount of tyranny by organized followers and by unhealthy leaders, we ask you to guide us into your truth. Give us the wisdom, courage, and strength to truly love and serve our fellow followers, especially those whom we choose to lead us. Show us the way, God, and give us the courage and strength to constantly become more effective in advancing the character and priorities of your Kingdom in every organization. May your will be done on earth as it is in heaven. Amen.

Questions and Issues

A. What are your working definitions of "effective following" and "effective leading"?

B. Why is it important to understand that leader and follower are situational roles that you play, not permanent elements of your identity as a person? What difference does it make?

C. To follow you must trust or respect the leader to some extent. Do leaders also need to trust followers? If so, in similar ways or differently? What might make the follower role and functions more variable and more difficult to see, fulfill, evaluate, depend on, and develop than the leader role?

D. In what ways do these two roles operate differently when they are part of family, friend, or volunteer relationships compared with workplace or other more formal organizational contexts? For example, do you tend to be more candid and consistent in these roles at home or in work and other external settings? Why?

E. The necessity of having a job of some kind to make a living, even if you are "self-employed," typically requires you to lead and follow in certain ways, regardless of how you might personally feel about or trust the other persons involved. How do you deal with the dissonance that can exist between personal and "organizational" relationships and perceptions of people?

F. At work and in other nonfamily organizations, what could make leading more visible, firmly defined, and stable than following? What makes followership so variable?

G. Have you ever needed to act or speak as a courageous follower confronting a leader? If so, what resulted from your action?

H. Given the highly varied and variable nature of followership, described here as varying degrees of different types of followership, what would be an effective approach to helping people be more effective at followership according to your working definition of effective following?

Kingdom Blessings for Your Organizations

O ne day as he saw the crowd gathering, Jesus used a hillside near Capernaum, presumably so more people could hear him, to present a long comprehensive description and explanation of the Kingdom of God. That message has come to be called the Sermon on the Mount, as recorded in the gospel records of Matthew and Luke. Jesus explained that the Kingdom of God is coming, that it first comes spiritually and personally in people who welcome it by faith, and that you can recognize the presence or absence of the invisible Kingdom by its visible effects or results.

No matter what your personal need or priority may be, being in the Kingdom and putting the Kingdom first meets your need and results in movement toward true health and fulfillment for you and thus for all the other lives you touch in every relationship and context. That kingdom principle means that organizations that advance kingdom conditions in their policies, values, and culture will be healthier for everyone involved and thus more likely to succeed by every righteous measure.

Jesus' Sermon on the Mount begins with what are called the Beatitudes, blessings that come from choosing to follow Jesus and serve his Kingdom as your highest priority. Each blessing is a promise to people with a specific need or desire. Taken together they can provide a way to think about the characteristics of an organization where at least some of the members are effectively acting to make the Kingdom of God the guiding model in the ongoing effort to make it healthy and successful. This condition occurs whether or not the owners or managers acknowledge Christ or his Kingdom.

When you seek first the Kingdom of God in an organization, God blesses you and your organization.

---

1.   If you acknowledge your spiritual poverty and weakness, when you seek first the Kingdom, God blesses you into being a person who feels and acts spiritually wealthy with abundant goodness that you can joyfully share.

2.   If you carry debilitating sadness from painful losses, when you seek first the Kingdom, God blesses you with complete healing that gives you joyful new strength to bring healing comfort to those who mourn.

3.   If you are deprived and disadvantaged because you are meek and humbly nonaggressive, when you seek first the Kingdom, you inherit every good thing in the whole earth.

4.   If you long fiercely for righteous justice in the world and work to achieve it, when you seek first the Kingdom, you will be satisfied by God's perfect justice in God's perfect time and way.

5.   If you consistently tend to seek and practice mercy, when you seek first the Kingdom, God will bless you with the joyful experience of his great mercy in every situation.

6.   If your heart's desire is for purity and perfection in all things, when you seek first the Kingdom, God will bless you with a clear vision of who he is.

7.   If you work for peace and consensus in every situation, when you seek first the Kingdom, God will bless you with the name and identity of a child of the heavenly father.

8.   If you are persecuted because you do what is right, and people insult you and falsely say all kinds of evil against you as you seek first his Kingdom, God is blessing you with confirmation that you are serving well in his Kingdom.

This recasting of the beatitudes offers one useful way to think about what the Kingdom of God could look like in your organization. People join an organization—a business, church, team, political party, university, agency, nonprofit, or any other kind of organization—with needs, fears, hopes, values, doubts, assumptions, and countless other realities common to the human predicament. Jesus looked at all those people coming to him with all those different deep realities, and he declared that by faith each person could experience the blessings of human fulfilment by fully embracing the Kingdom of God. Jesus predicted that the interdependent effectiveness of servant followers and servant leaders working as stewards of kingdom resources for kingdom ideals would bring the blessings of God to any organization. The beatitudes can enhance organizational health by prioritizing policies and actions that invoke God's blessing because they implement the values of his Kingdom. Followers, leaders, and organizations that truly enjoy God's blessing:

1. Realize their dependence on God.
2. Feel and express authentic empathy.
3. Demonstrate the kind consideration and teachable spirit of true humility.
4. Work for justice.
5. Show mercy.
6. Decide and act with pure motives.
7. Work for peace and unity.
8. Do the right thing even when it is costly, including being mocked and slandered for it.

In the same message about the Kingdom, Jesus provided another famously short and comprehensive principle for seeking the Kingdom. "Do for others what you would like them to do for you" (Matthew 7:12 NLT). When you pray for God's Kingdom to come and his will to be done on earth as it is in heaven, you logically also commit to act on your prayer. When you seek first the Kingdom of God by faith in Jesus Christ, you are blessed with fulfilment of what God had in mind when he created you. You do not take the blessings you seek by force or guile or at the expense of anyone else. You experience them by your faith in Jesus Christ that makes experiencing his Kingdom your top priority. And in his Kingdom, every unique person, made in God's image for God's glory and joy, is always called and blessed to personal fulfilment as an effective servant-follower. And sometimes also as an effective servant-leader.

Meditation

> When Moses' father-in-law saw all that Moses was doing for the people, he asked, "What are you really accomplishing here? Why are you trying to do all this alone while everyone stands around you from morning till evening?"
>
> Moses replied, "Because the people come to me to get a ruling from God. . . .
>
> "This is not good!" Moses' father-in-law exclaimed. "You're going to wear yourself out—and the people, too. This job is too heavy a burden for you to handle all by yourself. Now listen to me, and let me give you a word of advice, and may God be with you. . . . [S]elect from all the people some capable, honest men who fear God and hate bribes. Appoint them as leaders over groups of one thousand, one hundred, fifty, and ten. . . . Let the leaders decide the smaller matters themselves. They will help you carry the load, making the task easier for you." . . .
>
> Moses listened to his father-in-law's advice and followed his suggestions. He chose capable men from all over Israel and appointed them as leaders over the people (Exodus 18:14-25).

Moses was humble enough to listen to his father-in-law, and wise enough to learn to see the situation and his divine mandate in a different way. He fundamentally altered the dynamics of leading and following among the people he was responsible for.

Moses was an impressively prepared organizational leader. He had mastered the well-developed Egyptian system of governance and management. The Jewish people that God assigned him to lead had just finished four hundred years of enslavement under that Egyptian system of control. Both Moses and the people very understandably assumed that Moses was the only one among them who was capable of leading. In addition, he was a miracle-working prophet who received guidance directly from God. "Moses was considered a very great man in the land of Egypt, respected by Pharaoh's officials and the Egyptian people alike" (Exodus 11:3). There could have been a million or more people of Israel by the time Moses' father-in-law,

Jethro, arrived to talk with him, and Jethro could see the obvious reality that was invisible to Moses. He was overwhelmed and needed to create a hierarchical organization and delegate authority to others.

The account of this event is repeated at the beginning of the book of Deuteronomy as Moses reviews the lessons learned during their wilderness pilgrimage. The wilderness pilgrimage intentionally replaced the former leaders of tribes and families with a new generation who would follow their new leader, Joshua, as they moved into the land God had promised their ancestors centuries before.

But the account of this event in Deuteronomy has an important difference from the version in Exodus. In Exodus Jethro instructs Moses to select and appoint capable and honest men to be leaders. However, Deuteronomy adds a detail; Moses told the people to choose well-respected men from each tribe who were known for their wisdom and understanding. Then Moses appointed those nominees to be the leaders. Moses writes: "So I took the wise and respected men you had selected from your tribes and appointed them to serve as judges and officials over you" (Deuteronomy 1:13-14).

Moses wisely refined the guidance from Jethro and empowered the followers to choose their own leaders whom Moses then appointed, trained, and empowered. By delegating leadership to people who had trusting followers, Moses became a follower of those subordinate leaders, and he committed himself to their effectiveness. In return those leaders trusted Moses and strengthened his leadership as his followers.

Talking with God

Lord, how easily I forget that we are all followers who need to sense the whispers and nudges of your Holy Spirit to know who should lead us in each situation and what support they need from us. Too often I am silent and still when I should speak or act; and too often I speak or act before listening. How tempting it is to not "waste" the time and energy required to look at the situation from other perspectives, especially those of us who will be expected to do all the invisible work of followership that actually gets the job done.

Purify my deepest desires and motivations with the humility that lets me hear your voice and understand the way of life in your Kingdom. Help me remember that you give your wisdom to all of us, rarely to just one of us, and certainly not always only to me. We must listen and learn together. We need followers with your wisdom to choose leaders who have the character and competence to get all of us to the new condition we need. We want more people to follow Jesus, our Savior and King, and we want all of us to experience the blessings of your Kingdom as we learn to make it our top priority now as we long for its fulness.

Teach all of us to look for, recognize, and trust the wisdom you give when we practice effective following and leading together with all our different skills in all our different relationships, roles, and organizational situations. We want to keep on becoming more like Christ with successful organizations that are means of experiencing and advancing your Kingdom with all its blessings. Amen.

Questions and Issues

A. What current example could you identify that is similar to the humility and wisdom of Moses to learn from his father-in-law and delegate leadership authority to people who were recommended to him by the followers of those leaders?

B. How could your effective followership and leadership, grounded in kingdom stewardship, bring the blessings of the Kingdom of God to people affected by each of your organizations where you serve or are served?

Clarifying Note on Illustrative Cases

T he many illustrative cases presented in this book are based on my experience filling insider roles and formal positions as an organizational member and filling outsider roles, most commonly as a consultant, presenter, facilitator, observer, evaluator, or other type of change agent in 170 such assignments. Some of the cases are presented in the first person in my own voice, usually including explanatory commentary; some are first person in the voice of some other person where the perspectives and insights are their own; and some are third person accounts or descriptions. Except for my own firsthand personal accounts, most of the cases are composites created from two or more events or sources. And in all cases, including my own first-person accounts, no names are assigned to people to prevent identification and protect privacy. My home organizations may be stated or readily determined. The case illustrations are credible teaching devices that are grounded in factual reality.

The Church as an Organization

Churches are organizations and are grouped with other kinds of organizations in this book, whether it is a local congregation or a collection of congregations in a denomination, conference, or some other form of association. As such, a church organization needs to understand and practice the principles of healthy and successful organizational life. But it is *not* "just another organization." It is a unique kind of organization that exists for unique purposes in God's sovereign Kingdom plan during a limited period of time. All the members and the governing body (board, council, etc.) of a church organization must prayerfully understand and exercise their roles of following and leading, especially with regard to guiding the pastors and other positional "leaders" on staff, while also evaluating and holding them accountable. This book seeks to improve wise and effective following and leading for Christ and his Kingdom in every organization.

Notes

1. Randy Alcorn, *Heaven* (Carol Stream, IL: Tyndale House, 2004), 428.

2. Alcorn, *Heaven*, 362.

3. Alcorn, *Heaven*, 319.

4. Bernard M. Bass, *Bass Handbook of Leadership: Theory, Research, and Managerial Applications*, fourth ed. (New York: The Free Press, A Division of Simon Shuster, 2008). The ultimate comprehensive compendium of research and theory on leadership, with followership as a contributing component. The interpretive commentary and conceptual structures are valuable elements of this source. You may be able to rent or borrow this expensive resource.

5. Joseph C. Rost, *Leadership for the Twenty-First Century* (West Port, CT: Praeger Publishers, 1993), 44.

6. Edward J. Murphy, *The Power of Followership*, vol. 1, The Effectiveness Guide (Bellevue, WA: The Effectiveness Institute, 2012), 21.

7. Tom Atchison, *Followership: A Practical Guide to Aligning Leaders and Followers* (Chicago: Foundation of the American College of Healthcare Executives, 2004), 3. This thorough development of the interdependent nature of leading and following is set in the challenging context of the healthcare field, but it is easily adapted to many other similar situations involving highly qualified or credentialled professionals.

8. Michael Maccoby, *The Leaders We Need: And What Makes Us Follow* (Cambridge, MA: Harvard Business School Press, 2007), xvi.

9. Bass, *Bass Handbook of Leadership*, 8.

10. Robert Greenleaf, *Servant Leadership* (Mahwah, NJ: Paulist Press, 1977).

11. R. Scott Rodin, *The Steward Leader* (Westmont, IL: Intervarsity Press, 2010), 82.

12. Bruce Bueno de Mesquita and Alastair Smith, *The Dictator's Handbook: Why Bad Behavior Is Almost Always Good Politics* (New York: Public Affairs of the Perseus Books Group, 2011).

13. Barbara Kellerman, *Bad Leadership: What It Is, How It Happens, and Why It Matters*, (Cambridge, MA: Harvard Business School Press, 2004).

14. Tomas Chamorro-Premuzic, *Why Do So Many Incompetent Men Become Leaders? And How to Fix It* (Cambridge, MA: Harvard Business Review Press, 2019).

15. Maccoby, *Leaders We Need*, 93.

16. David Brooks, "The Follower Problem," *New York Times*, June 11, 2012.

17. Jean Lipman-Blumen, *The Allure of Toxic Leaders* (Oxford University Press, 2005).

18. Amitai Etzioni, *Modern Organizations* (Prentice Hall, 1964), 36.

19. Etzioni, *Modern Organizations*, 45–48, 61.

20. Bass, *Bass Handbook of Leadership*.

21. Joseph C. Rost, *Leadership for the Twenty-First Century*.

22. Warren Bennis, *On Becoming a Leader* (Boston: Addison-Wesley Publishing Co. 1989), 1.

23. Bennis, *On Becoming*, 5.

24. Atchison, p.184.

25. Tom E. Jones, *Doers: The Vital Few Who Get Things Done* (Washington, DC: WORx Publishing, 2017).

26. R. Scott Rodin, *The Steward Leader* (Chicago: InterVarsity Press, 2010), 17–18.

27. Tom Atchison, *Followership: A Practical Guide to Aligning Leaders and Followers* (Health Administration Press, a division of the Foundation of the American College of Healthcare Executives, 2004), 4–5.

28. Atchison, *Followership*, 231.

29. Atchison, *Followership*,163.

30.   Allen Hamlin Jr., *Embracing Followership: How to Thrive in a Leader-Centric Culture* (Bellingham, WA: Kirkdale Press, 2016). A great book for understanding, valuing, and enjoying the work of following and appreciating those who follow with exceptional grace, satisfaction, and effectiveness.

31.   Robert Kelley, *The Power of Followership: How to Create Leaders People Want to Follow and Followers Who Lead Themselves* (New York: Doubleday,1992), 236.

32.   Lipman-Blumen, *The Allure,* 136.

33.   Gene Dixon, *The Art of Followership: How Great Followers Create Great Leaders and Organizations* (Hoboken, NJ: Jossey-Bass, 2008), 162. See chapter 12, possibly the best chapter in what may be the most complete book on the interdependence of effective following and leading in healthy and successful organizations.

34.   Dixon, *The Art of Followership*, 158–59.

35.   Ira Chaleff, *The Courageous Follower* (Oakland, CA: Berret-Koehler, 2003).

SCAN HERE to learn more about Invite Press, a premier publishing imprint created to invite people to a deeper faith and living relationship with Jesus Christ.